SOFTWARE CERTIFICATION

Proceedings of the Centre for Software Reliability Conference entitled

Software Certification
held at the Penta Hotel, Gatwick, UK
13–16 September 1988

Members of the Centre for Software Reliability

T. ANDERSON, Centre for Software Reliability, University of Newcastle upon Tyne, UK

K. BENNETT, School of Engineering and Applied Science, University of Durham, UK

R. E. BLOOMFIELD, Adelard, London, UK

R. J. COLE, Glasgow College, Glasgow, UK

C. J. DALE, National Centre of Systems Reliability, Warrington, UK

M. DARNBOROUGH, IT Division, Department of Trade and Industry, London, UK

B. DE NEUMANN, Department of Mathematics, The City University, London, UK

J. E. DOBSON, Computing Laboratory, University of Newcastle upon Tyne, UK

N. FENTON, Centre for Software Reliability, The City University, London, UK

G. D. FREWIN, Standard Telecommunications Laboratories, Harlow, UK

C. H. GRIBBLE, Ferranti Computer Systems Ltd, Cwmbran, UK

L. N. HARRIS, British Aerospace Dynamics Group, Stevenage, UK

M. A. HENNEL, Department of Statistics and Computational Mathematics, University of Liverpool, UK

S. HINDE, Information Technology, Hemel Hempstead, UK

D. INCE, Open University, Milton Keynes, UK

A. KAPOSI, South Bank Polytechnic, London, UK

B. A. KITCHENHAM, Prestbury, Cheshire, UK

B. LITTLEWOOD, Centre for Software Reliability, The City University, London, UK

J. MCDERMID, Department of Computer Science, University of York, UK

R. MALCOLM, CAP Scientific, London, UK

P. MELLOR, Centre for Software Reliability, The City University, London, UK

M. MOULDING, Royal Military College of Science, Swindon, UK

M. OULD, Bath, UK

P. ROOK, Marlow, UK

S. STOCKMAN, British Telecom Research Laboratories, Ipswich, UK

J. G. WALKER, STC Technology Ltd, Newcastle upon Lyme, UK

A. A. WINGROVE, Farnborough, Hants, UK

R. WITTY, Software Engineering, The Alvey Directorate, Didcot, UK

SOFTWARE CERTIFICATION

Edited by

BERNARD de NEUMANN

Department of Mathematics,
The City University, London, UK

ELSEVIER APPLIED SCIENCE
LONDON and NEW YORK

ELSEVIER SCIENCE PUBLISHERS LTD
Crown House, Linton Road, Barking, Essex IG11 8JU, England

Sole Distributor in the USA and Canada
ELSEVIER SCIENCE PUBLISHING CO., INC.
655 Avenue of the Americas, New York, NY 10010, USA

WITH 19 ILLUSTRATIONS

British Library Cataloguing in Publication Data

Software certification (Conference; 1988; Penta Hotel)
    Software certification.
    1. Computer systems. Software. Reliability.
    Certification
    I. Title II. De Neumann, B. (Bernard) III. Centre for
    Software Reliability
    005.3

ISBN 1-85166-380-0

Library of Congress CIP data applied for

Printed in Northern Ireland by The Universities Press (Belfast) Ltd.

Preface

The safety and reliability of complex systems, and especially systems containing embedded software, has recently become a matter of public concern. The increasing incidence of computers in publicly available systems means that failures attributable to software will increasingly draw the attention of the public and, in the absence of any enforced standards, such failures will become increasingly catastrophic, and will act to the detriment of all. Thus it seems inevitable that the software engineering community will be required to become publicly accountable. One means of achieving this end is via certification.

This conference, the fifth in the annual CSR series, was a major milestone in the history of CSR, and it was thus felt that an important current issue would be an appropriate subject: the topic of certification seemed ideal. The intention of the conference organisers during the planning stage was to provide a forum in which current and future practices of the software certification process could be discussed and evaluated, especially in the light of the hotly debated appendices of the ACARD report of June 1986, 'Software—A Vital Key to UK Competitiveness'. Of course, our aims changed as time slipped by, but it is true to say that the 1986 ACARD report, and especially the more contentious portions, spawned the conference. The conference took place at the Gatwick Penta Hotel during 13–16 September 1988.

The value of any certification scheme depends upon its influence upon good practice, and an important part of this, of course, derives from the legal aspects and, in particular, their influence upon the actions of vendors, vendees and third parties. Since the legal aspects could become an important determinant in the future of software engineering, we begin by treating this subject. In Chapter 1, Ian Lloyd considers the extent of legal liability which may be incurred as a result of software malfunction. He also discusses the potential restrictive influence of contracts upon any such liability. In Chapter 2, Frédéric Copigneaux, after a general discussion on defining the term 'software certification', goes on to compare the merits of process certification and product certification. John Slater, in Chapter 3, reviews the current criteria for certification bodies, and then considers the work of the National Accreditation Council for Certification Bodies, and how the existing procedures may be extended to cover IT. Chapter 4, by Kevin Geary, begins by discussing the present and foreseeable certification requirements for safety critical software. A possible approach towards improving customer confidence in the applications of these techniques is advanced. In Chapter 5, Pat Neilan reviews the experiences of the National Air Traffic Services in approving embedded software for navigation. The paper goes on to describe NATS' evolving strategy, and its evaluation of modern techniques. In Chapter 6, Ian Spalding promotes the manufacturers' point of view on the certification process, and concentrates, in particular, upon airborne safety critical systems. Joan Hill, in Chapter 7, gives another vendor viewpoint, and in so doing discusses the problems of producing software that has to be certified. Certification in potentially hazardous industries is covered by Chris Dale in Chapter 8, where he discusses the research of the UKAEA and its relevance to future software certification activities. In Chapter 9, Andrew Bradley deals with the software aspects of the integrated systems approach, covering the role of formal methods, and verification and validation, to certification. Doug Miller discusses the application of statistical techniques to the problem of assuring and certifying ultra-high reliability, and assesses their feasibility in Chapter 10. He also suggests other roles in which statistical methods are important in assuring software quality. Finally, in Chapter 11, Bernard de Neumann discusses the application of the methodology of mathematical axiomatics to formal methods, and in so doing introduces the pointless example of continuous geometry. He then goes on to consider the strengths, weaknesses and foreseeable utility of the two topics.

The burden of my task as organiser of this conference was greatly lightened by the freely given, and much appreciated, valuable assistance of my colleagues who are members of the Centre for Software Reliability, in particular Chris Gribble, Joan Atkinson and Carol Allen. I am pleased to acknowledge my debt to them and, of course, to the speakers and delegates, who all contributed towards the success of the conference. I hereby express my sincerest appreciation, and beg to reward them all, most inadequately, with my humble thanks. I also place on record my thanks to all of the contributors for their timely production of the papers comprising this volume.

BERNARD de NEUMANN

Contents

List of Contributors

A. BRADLEY
British Aerospace Military Aircraft Division, Warton Aerodrome, Preston PR4 1AX, UK

F. COPIGNEAUX
Verilog, 150 rue N. Vauquelin, 31081 Toulouse Cedex, France

C. DALE
National Centre of Systems Reliability, United Kingdom Atomic Energy Authority, Wigshaw Lane, Culcheth, Warrington WA3 4NE, UK

B. DE NEUMANN
Department of Mathematics, City University, Northampton Square, London EC1V 0HB, UK

K. GEARY
Sea Systems Controllerate, Ministry of Defence, Foxhill, Bath BA1 5AB, UK

J. V. HILL
Rolls-Royce and Associates, PO Box 31, Derby DE2 8BJ, UK

I. LLOYD
The Law School, University of Strathclyde, Glasgow G4 0RQ, UK

D. R. MILLER
Department of Operations Research, School of Engineering and Applied Science, George Washington University, Washington DC 20052, USA

P. J. NEILAN
National Air Traffic Services, 45–59 Kingsway, London WC2B 6TE, UK

J. A. SLATER
Logica Consultancy Ltd, 64 Newman Street, London W1A 4SE, UK

I. N. SPALDING
Smiths Industries Aerospace and Defence Systems, Bishops Cleeve, Cheltenham, Gloucestershire GL52 4SF, UK

1

CERTIFICATION OF COMPUTER SOFTWARE
THE LEGAL ASPECTS

IAN LLOYD
The Law School
University of Strathclyde
Glasgow G4 ORQ

ABSTRACT

This paper describes the extent of legal liability which may be incurred by the producer and/or supplier of computer software in respect of damage suffered by a customer or a third party as a consequence of its improper operation. The extent to which this liability may be restricted or excluded by means of contractual techniques is outlined and the legal consequences arising from the introduction of certification procedures and quality standards are discussed.

1. INTRODUCTION

By certifying that a particular piece of software meets specified standards its producer and/or the certifying authority concerned may be taken to have made legally binding representations concerning its condition and suitability for its designated purpose or purposes. Such a situation may offer advantages to both supplier and customer. From the supplier's perspective, an accurate assessment can be made as to prospective liability, whilst the customer will benefit from a more specific and detailed statement as to the quality of the software than is to be found in the provisions of the general law. Nonetheless, a number of pitfalls lie in wait for those seeking to follow the certification road. At best these may result in any certificate being worthless whilst, at worst, it is possible that the supplier and/or certifying authority may incur civil or even criminal liability.

This paper will attempt, first, to describe the existing

legal requirements imposed upon a software producer and the
range of those to whom liability may be owed, second, to
outline the basic legal techniques by which liability may be
defined or limited and, finally, discuss those legal
requirements which may influence the nature and extent of any
certification procedures.

2. CONTRACTUAL LIABILITY

a. Computer Software - Product or Service?

In civil law a distinction is drawn between contracts for the
sale of goods and those for the supply of services. As with
the famous story of the attempt to describe an elephant - I
don't know what it is but I know one when I see one - most
lawyers would claim an ability to distinguish between the two
forms of contract but find it difficult to draw a principled
distinction between them. Essentially, this rests in an
assessment of the primary purpose of the transaction. If this
envisages the transfer of ownership of physical objects from
the seller to the buyer then the contract will be one of sale
of goods. If the intention is primarily that the supplier
will exercise skill and labour on the customer's behalf then
the contract will be one of services even though some
physical property will also change hands. If, for example, a
garage is engaged to carry out a service on a car this may
involve new parts being fitted to the vehicle. Having paid
for these, there is no doubt that the customer will become
owner of the parts. The prime purpose of the whole contract,
however, will be that the garage will exercise its mechanical
skills on the customer's behalf and the contract will be
characterised as one of services(1).

The extent of the supplier's liability in a contract for the
sale of goods is laid down in the Sale of Goods Act 1979(2).
This provides a number of terms which are to be implied, or
written into, any contract of sale. The most important of
these provisions are to be found in sections 13 and 14. These
state, respectively, that goods supplied under a contract of
sale must correspond with any description which may have been
applied to them and must also be of merchantable quality and
reasonably fit for any specific purpose or purposes for which
they are supplied.

In respect of the implied term as to description a major
problem is to determine which of the attributes allegedly
possessed by an object truly form part of its description. As
a general rule, laudatory terms such as "top quality", "first
class" or "excellent condition" will be regarded as

advertising puffs and will not be taken into account by the court in any subsequent legal proceedings alleging a breach of description. Any statement, however, that goods conform with specified standards or have been accredited by specified agencies or have undergone particular forms of testing will be regarded as descriptive. It may be noted that the Trade Descriptions Act 1968, which makes the issuing of a false description a criminal offence, specifically refers to claims that goods have been tested or approved by any person or that they conform with any standards(3).

Section 14 of the Act contains two implied terms as to quality. These will be written into any contract of sale in the absence of - and in some cases despite - any contrary terms specifically agreed between the parties. Its requirements that goods be of merchantable quality and fit for their purpose constitute two of the oldest legal formulations in current usage. The notion of merchantable quality, in particular, dates back several hundred years. Whilst this durability may be a tribute to the intrinsic soundness of the concepts their relevance to modern society may be criticised. In particular it has been argued that the requirements are more appropriate to simple products, readily susceptible to effective examination by a non-specialist than to the complex and sophisticated products of today's society(4).

Originally, the phrase 'merchantable quality' was defined by reference to concepts such as value for money and the resale value of goods supplied under the contract to a buyer who was aware of any hidden defects. The 1979 Act introduced a statutory definition which has served to blur the distinction between the two implied terms. Today, merchantable quality requires that goods must be:

> ".. as fit for the purpose or purposes for which goods of that kind are commonly supplied as it is reasonable to expect having regard to any description applied to them, the price (if relevant) and to any other relevant circumstances."(5)

whilst the second implied term states that:

> ".. where the buyer, expressly or by implication, makes known to the seller.. any particular purpose for which the goods are being bought there is an implied condition that the goods supplied under the contract are reasonably fit for that purpose whether or not that is a purpose for which the

goods are commonly supplied except where the circumstances show that the buyer does not rely, or that it would be unreasonable for him to rely on the seller's skill and judgment."(6)

These implied terms can be seen as introducing general and specific requirements that the goods be fit for their purpose. Although both lay stress on the functional acceptability of goods, recent cases make it clear that other, more subjective factors, will also be taken into account. This point was demonstrated in the case of Rodgers v. Parish(7) which furnishes an illustration of current judicial thinking in this regard. Mr Rodgers purchased a new Range Rover. The condition of the vehicle proved far from perfect. Water leaked in through the window seals, the paintwork was mottled, the gears were stiff, the engine was noisy and journeys were accompanied by a cacophony of rattles. In response, however, to the customer's claim that the vehicle was not fit for its purpose the seller argued that the purpose of a car was to be driven and that the present specimen was capable of being safely put to such a use. This argument was accepted by the judge at first instance but was unanimously rejected by the Court of Appeal which held that fitness for purpose required more than mere functional adequacy but encompassed also such matters as:

".. the appropriate degree of comfort, ease of handling and reliability and, one might add, of pride in the vehicles outward and interior appearance."(8)

To a considerable extent, similar criteria may be applicable in the case of computer software.

In the event that the statutory requirements are not met, the sellers will be held liable and the fact that the defect occurred in the absence of any fault on their part will be no defence. This point may be particularly apposite to computer software where products may frequently enter unexplored territory and where defects may not appear for some considerable period of time. Should these render the product unfit for its normal purpose or for any particular purpose specified by the customer the supplier will be held liable even though the defect may not have been susceptible of prior discovery.

By contrast, where a transaction is classified as relating to the supply of a service the supplier's liability is less onerous. Under the terms of the Supply of Goods and Services Act 1982, the supplier is charged with a duty to exercise reasonable skill and care in providing the service(9). A simple example relates to the conduct of a surgeon in operating on a patient. In the event that the patient dies it is obvious that the operation has failed to accomplish its purpose but the surgeon will only be held liable if it can be established that his performance fell short of the level to be expected of the average surgeon. Similarly, should software supplied as part of a contract for services prove defective, the supplier will be liable only if it can be shown that no reasonable supplier would have failed to discover and rectify the defects. In particular, it will be a defence to establish that the compilation process followed accepted industry standards.

It is clear from this brief analysis that it would be to the advantage of software suppliers for their transactions to be categorised as involving the supply of services. This point has been extensively litigated within the United States but has not, to date, exercised the mind of a British court(10). In the absence of decisive authority the best view would appear to suggest that standard software will be classed as a product requiring to comply with the Sale of Goods Act whilst the provision of custom designed software will be a service. From the perspective of the possible exclusion of liability or the legal implications consequent upon the introduction of a certification procedure, however, the distinction between products and services is of no practical significance.

b. Contractual Remedies

The customer's remedies in the event of a supplier's breach of contract are twofold. First, it may be argued that the seller's failure to comply with his contractual obligations justifies the buyer in rescinding or terminating the contract. This involves the return of the defective products to the supplier and the return of their price to the buyer. The difficulty with recission from the buyer's perspective is that the Sale of Goods Act provides that this right is lost when the buyer has retained the goods beyond such length of time as permits him to make a reasonable examination of the goods. The case of Bernstein v. Parson's Motors (11) demonstrates that this provision may operate against the customer. Bernstein purchased a new car. Four weeks later and after he had driven it for some 100 miles the vehicle broke down on a motorway sustaining substantial engine damage. It was subsequently discovered that at some stage during the vehicle's manufacture a blob of sealing compound had found its way into the lubrication system. It remained there, floating through the system, effectively constituting an incident waiting to happen until it ultimately caused a blockage resulting in the engine seizing up in a dramatic, expensive and potentially dangerous fashion.

Mr Bernstein attempted to rescind the contract only for the court to hold that his retention of the goods for a period of four weeks destroyed this right. The buyer, it was decided, was entitled only to such time as was necessary to make a general examination of the product. No account was to be taken of the nature and location of a particular defect. In this case, as will be the case with many software defects, the fault was not susceptible of easy identification, its existence only becoming apparent when a particular set of circumstances brought it into the open in spectacular fashion.

The fact that recission may be impossible does not serve to totally deprive the customer of rights under the Act. In the Bernstein case the court did hold that the car was unmerchantable but that Mr Bernstein's remedy lay only in damages. These represented the difference between the value of the vehicle in its defective state and its proper value as a functioning item, effectively the cost of putting the damage right.

In addition to being able to claim compensation for the diminished value of the product an agrieved customer will be able to demand compensation for any further loss which has reasonably sprung from the defect. Once again the appearance of the word "reasonably" serves to limit the extent of the supplier's liability. Under English law two kinds of damage can be identified as resulting from the supplier's breach of contract in providing goods which are not of merchantable quality or which are not fit for their purpose. Every supplier is liable in respect of those losses which could reasonably be forseen as a consequence of the supply of a defective product. This may be defined both by reference to any claims which may be made by the supplier as to the intended use of the product and to any requirements specified by the purchaser. In the event, for example, that due to a defect in its program, a computerised saw causes injury to its purchaser this will be regarded as a foreseeable consequence with the supplier being held liable for the loss. Where the particular loss suffered is less foreseeable, however, the supplier will only be liable in the event that he was specifically warned by the customer as to the possible dangers. The distinction between these two forms of damage is not susceptible of precise definition but generally where the claimed loss is one stage removed from the defect in the product actual knowledge will be required. This causes particular difficulties where the customers's claim reflects economic loss, often in the form of lost profits or opportunities. Recent litigation in the United States furnishes a relevant example of such a situation(12). Here, legal proceedings were instituted against the producer of a spreadsheet program. The customer in this case used the program in preparing a contract quotation. The contract was subsequently awarded but was subsequently alleged that, owing to a defect in the spreadsheet program, the quotation was uneconomically low and a claim lodged for the difference between the quoted price and what would be regarded as a reasonable figure for a contract of this nature. This action was subsequently withdrawn prior to judgment being delivered but it provides an illustration of the kind of problem which may result from increasing reliance upon the computer. Should similar proceedings be initiated in the United Kingdom it is likely that the claim would be dismissed on the basis that the loss was not sufficiently foreseeable.

In considering the extent of remedies in the event of breach of contract, a major limiting factor lies in the fact that only the party who has a contractual relationship with the supplier will be entitled to pursue a claim for compensation. Given the nature of many business organisations this will mean that a piece of software will be produced by one party, sold to one or more intermediary parties until the final sale to the ultimate customer. In the event that the software is defective there may follow a chain of actions in which each party seeks recompense for the loss suffered from the party with whom they have a contractual relationship(13). It may finally be noted that, save in the absence of any suitable contractual provision, the remedy for an agrieved buyer will take the form of some amount of monetary compensation. The buyer has no general right to require that the supplier repair any defect or that he supply a replacement for a defective product. It would appear from case law, however, that the seller's willingness to attempt to put any defects right will be a factor taken into account in determining whether goods are to be regarded as merchantable and fit for their purpose(14).

3. NON-CONTRACTUAL LIABILITY

a. Tortious Liability

The traditional counterpoint to the law of contract is found in the law of tort. Under this everyone, whether individual or company, owes a duty of care to avoid actions which are likely to cause harm to their neighbour. In the leading case of Donoghue v. Stevenson(15) the House of Lords held that the

manufacturer of a product owed a duty to the ultimate user of
that product. A similar conclusion was reached in relation to
services in the more recent case of Hedley Byrne v.
Heller(16). As is the position with the contract for the
supply of services, the standard of care is that of the
reasonable man operating within the particular profession. A
case which may be of relevance to the software industry is
that of the Lady Gwendolen(17). Here, a ship containing a
cargo of 'Guiness' was sailing from Dublin to Liverpool.
Thick fog shrouded the River Mersey but the ship proceeded at
full speed and, although the vessel was fitted with radar
equipment, the Master made no use of this. Inevitably, a
collision took place, the Lady Gwendolen ramming and sinking
another ship. Under the terms of the Merchant Shipping Acts a
ship owner is held strictly liable for damage caused by his
vessel. This liability is subject to statutory limits but
these do not apply in the event that negligence could be
established when the shipowner will be held liable for the
full cost of any damage which should reasonably have been
foreseen as likely to result from the negligence. In this
case the court held that the failure of the Master to make
proper use of the radar equipment provided constituted
negligence and, therefore, the owners were fully liable for
the damage caused by the collision.

Transferring these principles to the software field, it might
be argued that a failure to use any certification schemes or
verification procedures readily available to producers might,
in itself, furnish evidence of negligence in the event that
software proved defective.

The requirement that negligence be established against a
particular party serves to limit the application of the law
of tort. This area of the law may, however, assume
significance in two situations within the software field.
First, where defective software causes harm or loss to a
person other than its purchaser and, second, where the
customer purchases software from a retailer, the software
proves defective and causes harm but the seller, with whom a
contractual relationship exists, is no longer in business. In
this situation, a tortious action against the software
producer may provide the only viable remedy.

b. Product Liability

The introduction of a system of product liability is a novel
feature of our law and one which possesses significant
implications for software producers. As we have seen, where a
customer purchases goods, an action will lie against the
seller in the event that the goods are defective. There is no

need to establish fault on the seller's part. The Consumer Protection Act of 1987 which was introduced in order to ensure the UK's compliance with the terms of a European Community Directive(18) extends this 'no fault' liability to the manufacturer of a product which causes either physical injury or damage to other property(19). The basis for liability lies in a finding that the product is defective. The Act defines this as being where:

"The safety of the product is not such as persons generally are entitled to expect."(20)

The question arises once again whether software can be regarded as a product. The Government have commented to the effect that:

"Special problems arise with those industries dealing with products concerned with information such as books .. and computer software. It has been suggested that it would be absurd for printers to be held liable for faithfully reproducing errors in the material provided to them which by giving bad instructions .. indirectly causes injury."(21)

Against this it may be argued that the basis of the system is to introduce "no fault" liability and that no substantial distinction can be drawn between the printer or software producer described above and any other producer who is supplied with a defective component by a sub-contractor. In the American courts a distinction has been adopted dependant upon the fact whether the reader of a book or the user of a computer program might be expected to interpose his own expertise or reasoning between the text and its application or whether there would be blind and unthinking reliance upon its message. Thus, airline charts purporting to show the geography of the terrain surrounding airports and the approved navigational procedures were classed as a product and the publisher held strictly liable when these failed to indicate a mountain with disastrous consequences for the occupant of a plane(22). The court in this case also took account of the mass produced nature of the charts.

Even in situations, however, where custom software is required this will be installed on hardware and may be used to control the operation of physical components (for example a program designed to control the flight of an aeroplane). In the event that a defect in the software causes a malfunction it seems certain that the product as a whole will be considered defective and its manufacturer held strictly liable.

c. The State of the Art Defence

The scheme of product liability is sometimes referred to as introducing "no fault" liability. Effectively it offers an insurance scheme to the public whereby manufacturers will be held liable for any damage or injuries caused by their product without the injured party being required to establish fault on their part. As most members of the public will readily confirm, the amount of cover provided by an insurance policy will depend upon the size of the premium paid; whilst the insurance policy which is not subject to exclusions and exceptions exists only in the world of fairy stories. Product liability constitutes no exception to this rule. The price of product liability will be met by the mass of consumers in the form of increased prices (levied in order to compensate for the increased insurance premiums required to be paid by manufacturers), whilst the theoretical strictness of the liability is mitigated by the creation of a number of defences. The most controversial of these relates to the, so called, "state of the art" defence. Under the terms of the Directive it is generally provided that it shall be a defence for a manufacturer to establish that:

> ".. the state of scientific and technical knowledge at the time when he put the product into circulation was not such as to enable the existence of the defect to be discovered."(23)

It is further provided, however, that national legislatures may determine that this defence should not be available within their territory. This option has not been exercised by the United Kingdom, the Consumer Protection Act providing that no liability shall arise under product liability where it can be established that:

> ".. the state of scientific and technical knowledge at the relevant time was not such that a producer of products of the same description as the product in question might be expected to have discovered the defect if it had existed in his products whilst they were under his control."(24)

The extent of existing knowledge may, of course, be a matter of debate and dispute. Opinions may vary both as to the existence and scale of a potential risk and as to the efficacy of any techniques for detecting and eliminating it. The optimum solution may only become apparent in retrospect. The state of the art defence is likely to be of particular value to the manufacturers of pharmaceutical products where side effects may only became apparent after a substantial period of time, the Thalidomide tragedy providing an apposite scenario. Similar considerations may apply in the case of computer software and, here, the fact that industry standards and procedures have been designed and complied with may permit producers to enjoy immunity under this defence.

4. EXCLUSION OR LIMITATION OF LIABILITY

The above analysis demonstrates that software producers are exposed to a considerable degree of liability both to their customers and to others who may come into contact with their wares. In such a situation it is a well established legal technique to attempt to limit, or even to exclude, liability by means of an contractual clause or non-contractual notice. Examples of such clauses are legion, one relating to a popular word processing package being by no means untypical in providing that:

> " X gives no warranties with respect to the program
> licensed hereunder and all implied warranties,
> including warranty of merchantability and fitness
> for purpose, are hereby excluded."

Despite their undoubted popularity it is by no means certain that clauses such as this are legally enforceable. Two obstacles have to be overcome. First, it must be established that the customer was aware of the clause prior to purchasing the software. In many cases the exclusion clause is to be found in the terms of a licence which is contained in the packaging. This may not be seen until after the software has been purchased and, in such a case, it is unlikely that the clause will be effective. Even if the clause is timeously brought to the customer's notice the provisions of the Unfair Contract Terms Act 1977 come into play. These apply to both consumer and to business or commercial contracts. A consumer contract exists where the seller sells in the course of a business but the buyer does not act or hold himself out as acting, in such a capacity and where the goods are of a kind ordinarily bought for private use or consumption. In such a case, any attempt to restrict or to exclude any liability that would otherwise arise under the terms of the Sale of Goods or the Supply of Goods and Services Acts (and the remedies provided thereunder) is to be null and void(25). The provisions of the Consumer Transactions (Restrictions on Statements) Order 1976 extend this prohibition even further, rendering any such attempt criminal. In business contracts, the Unfair Contract Terms Act provides that any clause attempting to restrict or exclude liability will be effective only in so far as it is fair and reasonable(26). The question whether an exclusion clause is fair and reasonable will have to be determined by reference to the facts of an individual transaction(27). It is suggested, however, that any attempt totally to exclude the application of the Sale of Goods Act's provisions is unlikely to be favourably regarded by the courts. More benign consideration may be given to terms which seek to define or even to limit the extent of the supplier's liability or which provide alternative remedies to those provided under statute rather than simply attempting to exclude all forms of liability. Such a situation may well offer a favourable prognosis for the acceptance of certification procedures.

In relation to non-contractual liability the Act provides that no attempt may be made to restrict or to exclude liability for death or personal injury resulting from negligence(28). Any other form of liability may, however, be excluded subject to the provision of a suitable notice to this effect. This may take the form of a disclaimer notice which appears whenever the software is loaded or run. Such a tactic will, of course, be effective only where the third party uses the software. In the event, for example, that an accountant uses a defective accounting package supplied by a third party and, consequentially, produces inaccurate accounts thereby causing loss to his client, there will be no interaction between the client and the program and no possibility for any disclaimer to become effective.

5. CERTIFICATION OF COMPUTER SOFTWARE

a. The Legal Effect of Certification

Certification can refer either to the manner in which a product or service has been created or as to the condition or quality of the finished product. In either event, the act of certifying will generally be taken as a legally binding description of its quality. Under the Sale of Goods Act it is provided that goods must comply with any description which has been attached to them. A statement that software has been vetted by a particular certification process will be regarded as descriptive and in the event of the software failing to comply will constitute prima facie evidence of liability.

b. Certification Procedures and Statutory Standards

Within their own terms of reference certification procedures will be legally binding. If a supplier claims that his product has been produced in conformity with specified standards then that claim must be borne out in reality. This is a matter which may give rise to factual dispute but which should raise no legal issues of significance. The more substantial issue concerns the relationship between the terms of a certificate and the somewhat nebulous requirements of the Sale of Goods Act concerning the quality and fitness of goods. These are more extensive than is commonly realised. Although the attempt is frequently made to exclude their application by means of an exclusion clause or notice, the effectiveness of such tactics is by no means assured. Although few cases have yet come to court it is the writer's opinion that the majority of blanket exclusion clauses currently used in the software field would not satisfy the reasonableness criteria found in the Unfair Contract Terms Act.

In addition to being of doubtful validity the use of such exclusion clauses would also appear incompatible with the one of the primary goals of any certification scheme, that of promoting and enhancing customer confidence in the products involved. Nonetheless, particularly with standard software it may be difficult for a supplier to be aware of the particular use to which a customer intends to put it. Equally the consequences and cost of any defect may be totally disproportionate to the price received by the supplier. Given these facts it may well be reasonable for a certification system to co-exist with limitation of liability clauses. Whilst these cannot exclude liability in the event that a defective product causes physical harm due to the producer's negligence in its compilation, in the field of economic loss clauses imposing a ceiling upon the producer's liability or restricting his obligations to those of curing the defect or of supplying a replacement program are likely to be upheld by a court. In one case, albeit of little authority, a judge in the County Court at Exeter held invalid clauses in a film developing company's standard conditions of contract limiting liability in the event of mishap to that of supplying a replacement film(29). The basis for this decision was that the company did not offer its customers any element of choice and that provision should have been made for the customer to choose to pay a higher fee for the service and to receive greater compensation in the event of mishap. Whilst such a notion does recognise the economic realities underpinning legal liability the concept may be unduly sophisticated. At best it may be considered that the notion of a sliding scale of liability represents an idea whose time has not yet come.

Whilst the notion of limiting liability is compatible with the aims of a certification scheme the basic question remains when a product is to be considered defective. Whilst no certification scheme can provide absolute immunity against the risk of individual rogue products(30) an aim should be to ensure that products which match the certification specifications will also be regarded as complying with the general legal requirements. The incentive for suppliers to venture out from the comforting - if illusory - shelter of blanket exclusion clauses may be limited if, after demonstrating that their product conforms with the certification standards, a court were to be find against them under the terms of the Sale of Goods Act. Although, given the vague nature of legal criteria such as merchantability, this may not be an easy task it carries the potential to bring a welcome measure of certainty and predictability into the lives of all concerned and will facilitate the task of securing adequate insurance cover in the event of mishap. The impact of certification procedures may indeed be felt even by non subscribing producers in that, should a certification scheme command widespread respect and observance, they may be taken into account by a court in determining what may be considered a reasonable standard for software.

c. Certification Procedures

Within the United Kingdom there is little statutory provision applicable to the development and application of certification procedures. The best known examples of such procedures are the British Standards devised by the British Standards Institute. The Institute was established in 1901 as the Engineering Standards Committee and was incorporated by royal charter under its present name in 1929. Constitutionally, the BSI is an independent, non-profitmaking and non-political body and although it enjoys a measure of government sponsorship it remains within the private sector. A number of other certifying authorities also exist, for example, the British Electrotechnical Approvals Board and, of course, the Centre for Software Reliability can itself be regarded as filling such a role. By and large compliance with standards recommended by these agencies is a voluntary matter although increasingly in the consumer field, safety legislation requires that products comply with published standards. An example can be seen in the case of the Plugs and Sockets etc (Safety) Regulations 1987(31).

In terms of ensuring compliance with standards two approaches can be identified. First the certifying agency may devise and promulgate standards or procedures and leave the question of compliance with these to manufacturers. In this event any failure may expose the manufacturer to the risk of civil proceedings and possibly also to a criminal action alleging breach of the Trade Descriptions Act 1968. This statute makes

it a criminal offence to apply a false trade description to
goods or services. As has been stated, a claim that the
product complies with standards is regarded as descriptive. A
second approach is for the agency itself to vet either the
manufacturer's processes or the finished products with a view
to ascertaining their conformity. Should this inspection be
carried out negligently the certifying agency may be held
liable to any third party who suffers loss as a result of a
software defect that should have been identified by the
certification process.

At this level the promulgation of standards poses few legal
issues.In effect, the extent of compliance with any standards
which may be laid down will be dependent upon the contents of
the standards and the degree of esteem in which the
certifying authority is held both by those involved in the
relevant industry and by the public at large. In the event
that a scheme attracts recognition and support it will serve
as a valuable asset for the certifying authority and for
participating manufacturers. In this event there may well be
the desire to protect the attributes and features of the
scheme against imitation by non qualifying competitors.
Although the legal doctrine prohibiting "passing off" will
give the original user of an identifying mark or name rights
to interdict the use of this, or of similar and potentially
misleading insignia, such actions are complex and success can
by no means be guaranteed. A preferable course of action may
be to seek formal recognition of and protection for the
scheme. This can be achieved through registering the
distinctive features of the scheme, name and any design logos
etc., under the provisions of the Trade Marks Act of 1938.
This provides that:

> "A mark adapted in relation to any goods to
> distinguish in the course of trade goods certified
> by any person in respect of origin, material, mode
> of manufacture, quality, accuracy or other
> characteristic from goods not so certified shall be
> registerable as a trade mark."(32)

Applications for registration are to be made to the
Comptroller-General of Patents, Designs and Trade Marks. In
this event along with details of the trade marks a draft must
be supplied of the regulations under which it is proposed
that the scheme will be operated. These will be transmitted
to the Board of Trade which will determine:

> "(a) whether the applicant is competent to certify
> the goods in respect of which the mark is to be
> registered;

(b) whether the draft regulations are satisfactory; and

(c) whether in all the circumstances the registration applied for would be to the public advantage."(33)

Applying these criteria the Board of Trade may either accept the scheme with or without modification or reject it. The Board's decision will be binding upon the Comptroller-General.

The above analysis predicates an "arms length" relationship between certifying authority and producer. Under this, the certifying agency stipulates standards and/or procedures to be followed in the production of software, perhaps accompanied by vetting procedures and makes these available to anyone who wishes to adopt the specified criteria. Registration of a trade mark is only permitted in the event that this is the case, the Act providing that the trade mark owner must not carry on trade in the goods involved. It may be, however, that the roles of the certifying authority and of relevant producers cannot be so clearly differentiated. In the event, for example, that the agency is funded entirely by producers and if its standards are invoked only by these undertakings, the question may arise whether the agency should more properly be regarded as a trade association. If this is not the case further legal issues will arise. In particular, attention will have to be paid to the provisions of the Restrictive Trade Practices Act of 1976 and the activities of the Director General of Fair Trading.

The 1976 Act contains provisions relating to agreements made between competing firms. These may relate to the terms and conditions upon which goods or services are supplied. Included in these are any agreements as to:

".. the processes of manufacture which have been or are to be applied to goods.."(34)

Also covered under the legislation are, so called, "information agreements. This last category is designed to obviate the necessity to prove the existence of a formal agreement between firms as to their future conduct, applying in the situation where firms agree merely to furnish each other with information concerning their policies and practices. Finally, the legislation applies in the case of any recommendations which may be made by trade associations as to the terms and conditions upon which their members should do business. A trade association is defined for this purpose as a:

> ".. body of persons (whether incorporated or not) which is formed for the purpose of furthering the trade interests of its members.."(35)

In the event that competing firms agree that their products will be developed according to agreed criteria and will meet specified standards, it is clear that some element of customer choice may be removed. In this sense the agreement will be restrictive and, as such, will come within the province of the restrictive trade practices legislation. Every agreement to which the Act applies requires to be registered(36). Application for registration is made to the Director General of Fair Trading who is charged with the task of compiling a register of the existence and scope of restrictive agreements. Prima facie, upon receiving such notification, the Director is obliged to refer the agreement to the Restrictive Trade Practices Court with a view to this tribunal making a decision as to whether the agreement should be declared invalid or upheld as being in the public interest. At the stage of an agreement being adjudicated upon by the court the chances of its being upheld are small. A much more hopeful avenue is made available through the fact that the Director may refrain from referring an agreement if he considers that the restrictive elements "are not of such significance as to call for investigation by the Court."(37) The consent of the Secretary of State will be required for such a course of inaction. In the longer term it is relevant to note that the Restrictive Trade Practices Act exempts from its scope agreements relating to agreements as to:

> ".. standards of dimension, design, quality or performance"

where these are:

> ".. standards or arrangements for the time being approved by the British Standards Institution or standards or arrangements prescribed or adopted by any trade association or other body and for the time being approved by an order of the Secretary of State made by statutory instrument."(38)

In the absence of such approval, reliance will have to be placed upon the Director General exercising his power to initiate a waiver of referral. To date, this has been exercised in the case of a number of codes of practice drawn up by trade associations specifying the standards expected of members of those associations in their dealings with the

public. Although the purpose and legal status of a code of
practice are not identical to those surrounding a
certification procedure the similarities are such that it
might be anticipated that similar considerations will apply
in determining their acceptability and validity. Two
conditions have been imposed upon trade associations or
similar bodies seeking to introduce a code of practice. First
that the code should not derogate from the legal rights
granted, whether by statute or otherwise, to the purchasers
of a product or service. The impact of this is more readily
seen in the consumer field. Here, exclusion clauses are
frequently prohibited and, consequently, a manufacturer or a
retailer's "guarantee" offering to repair or replace
defective products within a specified time period is subject
to the further provision that:

> "Nothing in this guarantee is to be taken as
> restricting or excluding the application of any
> legal rights whether statutory or non-statutory in
> origin."

The effect of this is that a customer having a complaint
about the quality of goods or services provided will have the
option of pursuing the complaint either under the provisions
of the code of practice or under those of the general law.
Although exclusion or limitation clauses may be more
acceptable in the case of commercial contracts the existence
of the requirement of reasonableness suggests that the
Director General would look askance at the terms of any
document which attempted to exclude all or an excessive
degree of liability. The point must also be made that whilst
the use of exclusion clauses by individual suppliers may be
upheld as fair and reasonable, the existence of a common
policy in this regard may not be so regarded.

The second requirement for any form of agreement to receive
the Director General's blessing can be briefly stated. The
terms must offer some benefit to customers. A certification
scheme, in other words must be worth more than the paper it
is written on.

6. EUROPE AND 1992

With the introduction of the single European market in 1992
any remaining barriers to trade between member states must be
removed. Product standards can effectively serve to inhibit
trade between member states and, as such, may require
modification. Whilst the burden of complying with the legal
requirements will primarily fall upon national governments,

voluntary certification procedures may be indirectly affected by the new regime. Any establishing agreements might be challenged under the European Communities competition laws whilst the existence of any significant discrepancies between the certification procedures applied in the various member states could result in pressure for the introduction of community standards in this area. Whether this would mark a positive or a retrograde step would, of course, depend upon the nature of the standards.

7. CONCLUSION

The above presentation has, perhaps inevitably, concentrated upon the difficulties that may be encountered in any certification procedures. It is clear, however, that well thought out and operated certification procedures offer substantial benefits to all those involved in the manufacture and supply of computer software. The views expressed in the White Paper "Standards, Quality and International Competitiveness"(39) demonstrate the government's acceptance of the benefits offered by voluntary certification schemes and their willingness to assist with their establishment and operation. Given that the enforcement of competition policy is a matter of politics as much as of law this is a by no means insignificant factor. Despite this apparent blessing, certification schemes remain to some extent in a state of legal limbo. Given the inability of lawyers to agree on on some of the basic questions concerning the nature and extent of a supplier's liability it would be unreasonable to expect suppliers to arrive at definitive or instant solutions. The potential benefits of certainty and precision offered by a successful scheme must make the process worth the effort. A genuine effort to provide for an equitable allocation of risk between supplier and customer is unlikely to face insurmountable legal hurdles.

NOTES

1. An indication of the difficulties and uncertainties involved in this area can be gauged from the fact that faced with contracts under which dental laboratories agreed to make sets of false teeth; one court found a contract of sale and, another, a contract for the provision of a service.

2. This statute essentially re-enacts the provisions of the Sale of Goods Act of 1893, a statute which itself attempted to restate the existing legal provisions in this area.

3. ss. 1-2.

4. The Law Commission in a recent report have recommended that the Sale of Goods Act's implied terms should be replaced by new formulations which would take specific account of factors such as the presence of minor defects and the durability reasonably to be expected of goods.

5. s.14(6).

6. s.14(3)

7. [1987] 2 W.L.R. 353.

8. Ibid p.359.

9. s.13.

10. For a review of recent United States developments in this area see Smith Suing the Provider of Computer Software (1988) 24 Williamette Law Review 743-765. Although the parallels between the United States and the British legal positions are not exact, both jurisdictions retain the notion of merchantability as a vital criteria in assessing liability under a contract for the sale of goods.

11. [1987] 2 All E.R. 220.

12. Cummings v. Lotus. It is relevant to note that IBM had initially been joined as defendants in this case. The action against them was dismissed at an early stage because of the effectiveness of the exclusion clauses contained in their standard conditions of sale.

13. The case of Godley v. Perry [1960] 1 W.L.R. 9 illustrates this point. Here, a boy was injured by a defective catapult which he had purchased from Godley and obtained damages in respect of these. Godley in turn sued Perry, the wholesaler from whom he had obtained the catapult seeking, and obtaining, reimbursement of these costs.

14. Millers of Falkirk v. Turpie 1976 S.L.T. (Notes) 66.

15. [1932] A.C. 579.

16. [1964] A.C. 465.

17. [1965] P. 294.

18. Directive 85/374/EEC.

19. s.2.

20. s.3.

21. Implementation of the EC Directive on product Liability - an explanatory and consultative note. Department of Trade and Industry. November 1985.

22. Saloomey v. Jeppesen (1983) 707 F. 2d 671.

23. Art.7.

24. s.4(1)

25. s.7(2).

26. s.7(3).

27. The Act contains, in Schedule 2, an illustrative list of factors which may be taken into account by a court in determining whether an exclusion clause should be considered reasonable.

28. s.16.

29. Woodman v.Photo-Trade Processing Ltd. (May 7 1981).

30. A warning note is sounded in this regard by the case of Retail Trading Standards Association v. Downland Bedding Co. (1959). Here a bedding manufacturer claimed that his product complied with

appropriate British Standards. A single product failed so to do yet the manufacturer was prosecuted and convicted on the basis of making a false claim concerning his product. Changes in the law introduced in the Trade Descriptions Act of 1967 make it unlikely that a single lapse will now result in prosecution but a producer will still have to establish that reasonable vetting procedures were introduced to the manufacturing or production processes.

31.   S.I. 1987. No. 603.

32.   s.37

33.   Schedule 1.

34.   s.6(1)(e).

35.   s.43(1).

36.   s.1.

37.   s.21.

38.   s.9(5).

39.   Cmnd 8621, 1982.

2

Software Process and Product Certification.

by

Frédéric COPIGNEAUX
VERILOG

150 Rue N. Vauquelin
F 31081 Toulouse Cedex
Tel : (+ 33) 61 40 38 88

Abstract :

Certification can be defined as an official assessment of equivalence between the specified and the actual service given by the software and/or system. There are basically two ways of certifying software : the indirect "process certification" and the promising "product certification".

Process certification is an indirect way of certification working in the following way :
- the certifier and the developer of software agree on a development methodology, the stringency of which is a function of the criticality of the software,
- this methodology is applied by the developer,
- the certifier checks that the methodology is effectively applied.

This "process" certification has been in use for some time (DO 178-A in Aeronautics ; Health and Safety Executive in the U.K.).

Product certification is defined as the direct assessment of the adequacy of the actual service versus the specified service. It is supported by the current advances in software engineering technology, and comprises three steps :

- precise identification, at the specification level, of the functional characteristics of software and of the non–functional attributes necessary for its intended use : reliability, maintainability, security, etc...
- measurement (quantitative) and examination (qualitative) of the same functional characteristics and non–functional attributes at the code and actual service level,
- multi–dimensional assessment of the equivalence between the two sets of attributes.

Although the reliability levels that can be demonstrated today by this certification technique are not high enough for high criticality applications, this way is promising because it is in compliance with the actual trends in software development technology. The fact that it can be automated also makes it economically attractive for widespread use.

The Esprit project SCOPE is aimed at developing and unifying software certification on the european scale. The development of a comprehensive and realistic technology for software product certification is one of its major objectives.

1. Software certification

This introduction comprises two parts. The first one is devoted to the definition of certification and the second one to its applications, both traditional in high criticality environments, and, more recently, to its potential advantages for the general software community.

1.1 Definition

The definition of certification by the IEEE < IEEE-83 > is :

> The process of confirming that a system, software subsystem, or computer program is capable of satisfying its specified requirements in an operational environment.

This definition refers to the actual certification tasks, but it does not take into account the final purpose of certification which is to give "confidence" in the product. This confidence is needed by the end user of the software, traditionally for its economic impact, but more acutely for compliance with regulatory constraints. The basic scheme is the following :

– a software producer,

– and a software consumer in need of confidence...

It is clear that confidence can only be attained if there is a third independent party, on which both the producer and consumer can rely, whose judgment is accepted by both and who can settle the disputes. The traditional implication of regulatory agencies into product safety leads to this amended definition of certification < SCOP-88 > :

> The process of product evaluation either by an official regulating body or an independent third party to establish that it complies with all necessary requirements, regulations and standards.

This definition has added two important components : the third independent party, and the regulatory implication. This implies that the basic scheme is now altered and incorporates the third independent party in which both the producer and consumer of software have trust.

1.2 Purpose

What is the purpose of software certification ? Historically, it is an extension of system certification for this has been existing for a long time. In safety critical applications such as aeronautics, nuclear power plants, etc... national and/or international regulations require the designers of such systems to satisfactorily demonstrate a significant level of product safety. This is generally treated with a probabilistic approach, reliability being the basic concept.

This certification process is mandatory before commissioning the product. It is a very complicated and costly process : the general estimation for civil aviation sets the costs of certification in the same order of magnitude that the actual design of a new aircraft.

Its benefits are evident : although no one could ever say that an aircraft was ever designed to be unsafe, the regulatory evolution, sometimes alas in consequences of severe accidents, tends to significantly rise the global level of confidence.

This in turn tends to be a "commercial" argument as airlines will require aircrafts to be certified to the latest amendment of the regulation, and that aircraft manufacturers will also emphasize on having their products certified to the latest and more stringent requirements.

As far a software is concerned in such systems, it is only a component. The basic need is the certification of the system and not that of the software, although specific software certification methodologies have been developed for this purpose.

In the mean time, software has also grown as a product of its own. For the kind of service delivered by these software products, there are actually no regulatory constraints although some are emerging (security). The producers and consumers are therefore not concerned with the benefits and burden... of certification. On the other hand, they only know too well the impact of software malfunction. The forthcoming european open market of 1992, and the product liability laws to be passed are also making this concern more acute.

This leads the software community to considering software certification as a possible solution to the problem by defining a procedure granting the certified software an **officially recognized seal.** This will be :

- a guarantee for the customer that the software possesses a certain set of well defined attributes that makes it suitable for its intended use,
- a protection for the producer against costly legal suits by the customer.

This general concept is illustrated on figure 1.

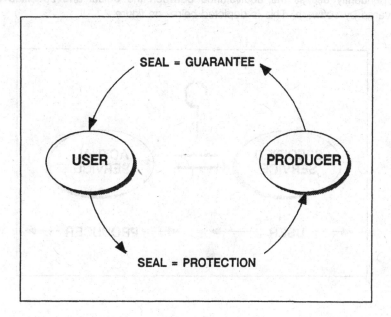

Figure : 1

If software certification is to be extended to all types of software, there is a need for efficient certification technology. This technology must address all types of software, including of course the high criticality domain. The rest of this paper reviews the different methodologies that can be used.

2.Certification techniques

If we refer to the definition of certification, the final objective of certification is to independently assess the equivalence between the actual and specified service delivered by software. This is depicted below on figure 2 :

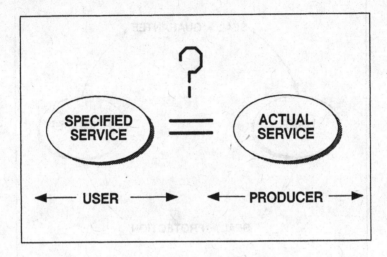

Figure 2

If we then consider that software is characterized by two sets of attributes :

- functional attributes positively describing the expected service. This set of attributes is precisely defined in the specifications which must be based on the service "expected" by the consumer. Where applicable, existing regulatory constraints will add functional features to the software. These must be taken into account for certification ;

- non-functional attributes such as reliability, maintainability, security. Here again, these requirements both stem from the consumer and in some cases from the regulations.

Both these attributes will be incorporated in the specifications.

The development process for software assures that the product is developed to comply with its specifications. The overall process is regulated by software quality assurance.

The purpose of the independent certification agency is now to assess the whole process as depicted on figure 3 :

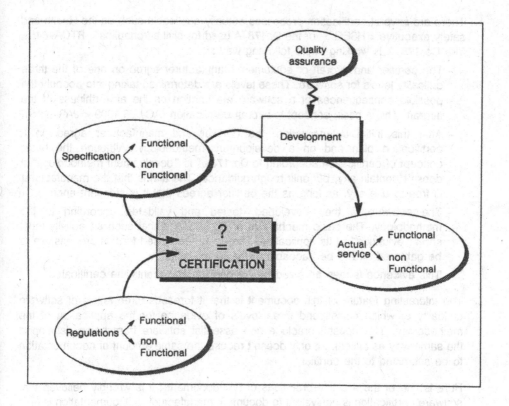

Figure 3

Historically, as software was perceived as immaterial, the first effective way to certify software was to rely on the thoroughness of its development methodology. This led to the indirect certification method : **"process certification"**.

There is however, another possibility which is to directly assess the equivalence of functional and non-functional attributes of software at the level of its specifications (specified service), code and behaviour (actual service). This is **"product certification"**.

2.1 Process certification

The general principle on which this certification technique is based is that the quality of software is in direct relation with the stringengy of the development method used. So the idea is to give the certificate to the software only if an adequate methodology has been used for its development.

This is very indirect in nature for the only thing one can be sure of in the end is that the methodology has been used... There are no direct implications of the software.

There are several certification processes actually applicable such as the Health and safety executive < HSEG > or the Do178-A used for civil aeronautics < RTCA-84 >. The Do 178-A is working in the following way :

- The certifier and aircraft or equipment manufacturer agree on one of the three criticality levels for software. These levels are determined taking into account the possible consequences of a software malfunction on the airworthiness of the aircraft. This a basic concept in aircraft certification (ACJ 25.1309 < JAR-86 >),

- After this initial categorization, the certifier and manufacturer agree on a certification plan and on a development methodology. Although the basic concept of certification according to Do 178-A is "development methodology" it doesn't contain any, but only rough guidance. The aim is that the manufacturer is free to use any, as long as the certifier agrees that it is stringent enough,

- The software is then developed, tested and validated according to the methodology. The basic mechanism of Do 178-A is that such an activity must show "evidence" of its application. The documents used for this process are to be gathered and to be traceable to the exact tasks,

- This evidence is then analyzed by the certifier who grants the certificate.

The interesting feature of this document is that it foresees three levels of software criticality to which correspond three levels of evidence for the application of the methodology. This doesn't preclude non-essential software from being developed the same way as critical... it only doesn't require the same amount of documentation to be submitted to the certifier.

Here is one of the mis-interpretations of this document : it is wrongly believed that software certification is equivalent to document manufacture... Documentation is only the evidence : it must therefore be the actual documentation used and not one "made on purpose".

This has been the main pitfall in the application of the first version of the Do 178, the certifier were either given nice looking documents that had only loose connections with the product, or buried under vast amounts of computer listings... This has been corrected with the Do 178-A which puts the emphasis to the access to information via the use of various summaries and traceability tables and matrixes.

Variants of this approach is "supplier certification" in which it is checked that the developer of software employs an officially recognized methodology, independently of any product. All the software produced by this supplier is then granted the certificate.

The main limitations of this approach are the following :

- there is little quantitative assessments of the software, and more generally, this approach doesn't guaranty much coverage for the non-functional aspects of software,
- it is very costly. The estimated cost differences for the manufacturer between Do 178-A levels of criticality is 4. On the other hand, the certifier will also be submitted to the same effort differences, and to the resulting cost differences.

One possible answer to this problem is supplier certification in which the certificate is granted to the manufacturer for all its product... but then there must be an absolute confidence between the certifier and manufacturer.

Apart from the level of effort implied, the high cost of such a certification process is due to the fact that it cannot be automated because the basic certification action is auditing...

2.2 Product certification

The basic principle is to directly assess the adequation of the actual service to the specified service, both in terms of functional and non-functional attributes. It is pictured on the figure below :

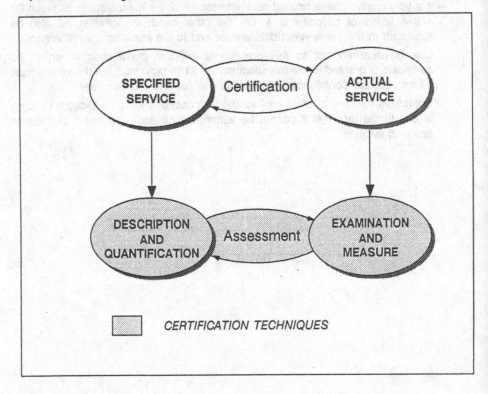

Figure : 4

Product certification comprises the following items :
- Assessment of equivalence between specified and actual service,
- Examination and measurement of the actual service,
- Description and quantification of the specified service.

2.2.1 Assessment of equivalence

In general, assessment is the determination to which extent one or several agreed, required or expected conditions for an object have been fulfilled. The assessment process is done by comparing given values for quality factors (target) with actual values for quality factors (obtained by measurement and/or examination) of an object (or several objects). Assessment results in ranking statements, such as : program X is more efficient than program Y, or : the actual state of an application concept is more complex than its target state.

Quality assessment requires :
- quality measurement and/or examination (actual quality graph) as well as,
- specification of requirements (target quality graph).

2.2.2 Examination and measurement of the actual service

It is the aim of examination and measurement to assess the actual service. The object to be investigated is analysed on the basis of the factors and characteristics defined in the quality model. Targets are required to enable one to assess the object on the basis of the information obtained. Roughly, we can say that :
- examination is the analysis of qualitative aspects, and,
- measurement is the analysis of quantitative aspects.

Examination : the qualitative analysis

A qualitative analysis can be done by analyzing the description (textual analysis), by interpretation and execution :
- Textual analysis is applicable to all objects. It produces information on the syntax structure of the object. *Inspection* and tools of *static analysis* can be used,
- Interpretation is applicable to all interpretable objects. It produces information on the algorithm the object includes. Applicable methods are *inspection, symbolic execution* and *verification*,
- Execution requires executable objects. It produces information on the dynamic behaviour of the object, i.e. on results, operations, etc... Methods to be used are those of *dynamic analysis*.

Measurement : the quantitative analysis

Quality measurement should be regarded as the determination of the values of the quality factors of an object. This is achieved by assigning numbers to each quality factor. This assignment has to be done such that relations between objects are mapped homomorphically onto real numbers.

It is necessary to derive from the world of observation those quantities of software that are easily measurable, i.e. that can be mapped onto elements of the world of numbers maintaining the specific relations. The problem is, however, how to obtain suitable quantities and how to put them into relation with the quality factors to be described. Therefore, a quality model is required as basis. This quality model defines and decomposes the relevant quality factors and determines their interrelations.

2.2.3 Description and quantification of the specified service

Three main type of specification techniques are currently used today. These techniques differ in their degree of formalism.

The less formal are the plain language specification whose drawbacks are well known : incompleteness, ambiguity, and incoherence.

Numerous specification methods have been developed to overcome this problem. They can be partitioned between formal and semi-formal methods. The former (FDM, HDM, GYPSY, AFFIRM, VDM,...) are proof oriented. These methodologies are supported by sophisticated tools (theorem provers) and their use is difficult and time consuming. They should be constrained to highly critical systems parts.

Structured analysis methods (IDEF, PSL/PSA, SREM....) provide an intermediate level of formalism in the specification. This formalism is not sufficient to support "mathematical proofs of correctness" but it allows for completeness and coherence verification, and for rapid prototyping.

In any case, specification leads to the characterization of the product in terms of:
- functional characteristics such as : performances, etc...
- non functional characteristics of the project such as : safety, security, reliability, etc...

Technology todays exists, at least in some domains, to successfully address this phase and produce an usable "reference" to which the actual service of the software can be compared.

2.2.4 Conclusion

Product certification is a rather new idea but its definition is clear and takes advantage of the recent advances in software engineering technology such as :
- the modeling of software quality and in general of non functional attributes such as reliability,
- metrication,
- formal and semi-formal specification techniques.

It nevertheless requires a lot of studies and experiments, and evaluation before being enforced. One of its greatest potential advantage is that is can be automatized to a large extent. This makes it highly attractive from an economical point of view.

3. The Esprit project SCOPE

Esprit project are a very suitable institution to conduct the applied research and development work necessary for enforcing software certification in general, and product certification in particular.

In accordance with the beneficial consequences of certification upon the software community, the ultimate goals of the project are to :

- Clarify the supplier to customer relationships by defining procedures enabling the granting of a "seal" to the software when it complies with a certain set of attributes,
- Develop new efficient and cost effective certification technologies for the granting of this seal,
- Promote the use of modern software engineering technologies to be used during the development of the software and contributing to the delivery of the seal.

This will assure a breakthrough in the industrialization of software production by giving an incentive to the producers of software to use innovative technologies and to cooperate with the developers of this technology.

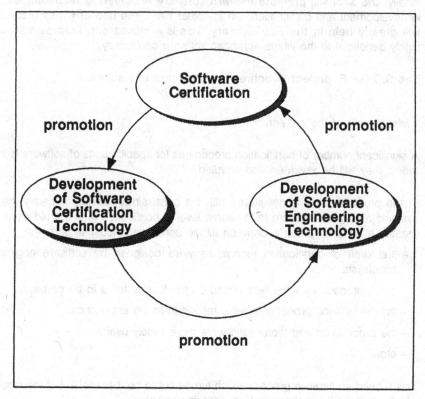

Figure : 5

All the objectives are linked together in the following way as depicted on figure 5 :

- The delivery of a seal assuring that the certified software possesses a minimum set of precise, and where relevant, quantified attributes will :
  . help the customer choosing the right software according to its intended use,
  . help protect the supplier against suits by the user if the software is used according to its limitations.

- New, efficient and cost effective certification technologies will be developed for this project. These techniques and tools will put the emphasis on direct measurement of the software attributes. They will derive from advanced R & D works actually underway in software engineering. The associated procedures will precisely define, for each type of software and according to its final use, the techniques and tools to be used. This will assure the cost–effectiveness of the certification process.

- Regarding the development process of software, modern techniques and tools will be designed so as to help the certification process. Again, these techniques and tools will derive from the advanced R & D works. This will assure the industrialization of the software development process.

Finally, **the seal will promote modern software engineering technologies,** both in development and certification. On the other hand, **the use of these techniques will greatly help in the seal delivery.** This is a closed loop process that will be highly beneficial to the whole european software community.

The S.C.O.P.E. project is entirely build around this scheme.

3.1 Mechanism of the project.

A significant number of certification procedures for specific uses of software is in use today. they will be reviewed and adapted.

These procedures were developed with the constraint of having to certify the new systems relying on software to the same level of confidence than the old ones. This created a dynamic process between all the concerned industrial partners:

- first draft of certification techniques were designed by software engineering specialists,
- these procedures were field–tested on the first systems to be certified,
- the certification procedures were refined from the experience,
- the procedures and techniques were more widely used,
- etc...

This formed an iterative process which turned out to be beneficial, but the results of which are actually confined to high criticality software.

The main idea in the S.C.O.P.E. project is to repeat this process for :
- all types of software,
- product certification techniques.

3.2 Main characteristics of the project.

The main characteristics and objectives of this project are:

Field validation of the proposed certification technologies :

It is proposed to repeat the process that led to the successful achievement of the existing certification procedures. This implies the following tasks :
- definition of the certification procedures, among existing ones and/or definition of new ones,
- experimental validation,
- use of a data base to gather and analyze the results of the test cases,
- evaluation of the results,
- modification of the procedures, or release for use,
- iteration of the process for other types of software....

This process is illustrated on figure 6.

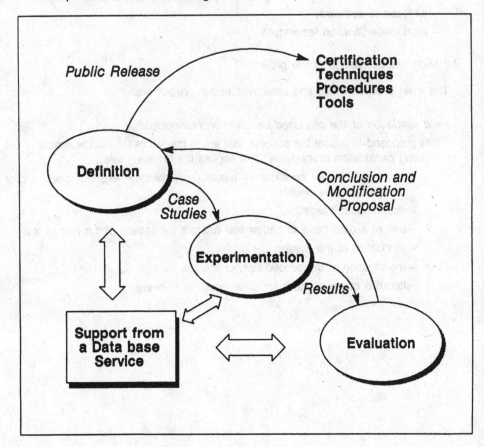

Figure : 6

Technical innovation :

The existing certification procedures and techniques are mainly "process" certification techniques. Although effective, they are costly and require an heavy workload in audits, reviews, etc... that cannot be easily automated. One of the goal of this project is to **promote product certification technologies.** Although it is clear that these techniques cannot today solely address the high criticality software, it is anticipated that they can give a significant gain in low and middle class applications.

Besides, there is the opportunity to use in the real world some of the sophisticated techniques (formal or semi-formal specifications techniques) that have currently only been used in high criticality, research or other limited circles. A gain in the ability to assess the conformance between **specified and expected service** is clearly anticipated from the use of these techniques.

Wide european coverage :

For the results of this project to be largely accepted and used by the european software community, it is necessary that the community participates to the design and validation of this technology. This implies the incorporation of different partners in this project :

- partners representative of the whole european software community such as software engineering specialists, test-laboratories, software producers, etc...
- a large geographical distribution of the partners.

Continuation of other projects :

This project will take advantage of both the results and the mechanisms used in previous european projects such as REQUEST. In this case, the data base mechanisms, and the administrative system which are used for the data collection can be either repeated straight away or incorporated in this project.

Coordination with the standardization organizations :

It is a necessity for this project to work in cooperation with the european standardization bodies. This project having an important practical aspect with the experimental validation of the techniques on case-studies, it is complementary of the efforts of these bodies which aim at defining regulations and standards.

A cooperation with the european on-going Conformance Testing Services (C.T.S.) is also anticipated for this program has outlined the importance of certification.

Coverage of the legal aspects :

The project objective of establishing criteria and methods for the certification of software should result in the development of industry standards. It is an objective of this project that these standards, leading to the granting of a seal to certified software, will effect the legal rights and obligations of those producing, selling and using items of software. A full assessment of the extent of such rights and duties would require a detailed investigation of the laws prevailing in each of the member states of the European Community. Fortunately, although national legal systems within the European Community vary in matters of detail a common conceptual core can be identified in this area.

The legal implication of S.C.O.P.E. would therefore be that the resulting certification procedures are mutually recognized by all states, and at least, have no features preventing this.

3.3 Project organization.

According to the previous objectives the organization of the project is the following as depicted on figure 7 :

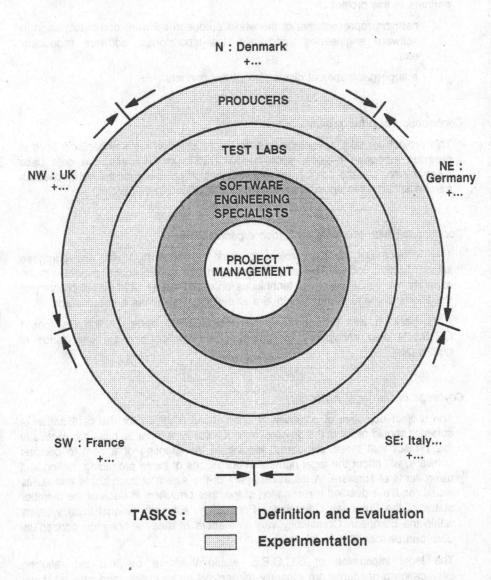

TASKS : Definition and Evaluation

Experimentation

Figure : 7

- **Management of the project** : this part should be kept small for efficiency relying on one representative per country;
- **Software engineering specialists** defining and evaluating the certification procedures and techniques;
- **Test-laboratories** participating in the certification procedure so as to assess its operational feasibility;
- **Software producers** participating in the experiments.

It is important that the project be sufficiently large so as to cover the objectives. There is typically a critical mass effect in terms of :
- number of experimental case-studies,
- number and type of partners,
- geographical distribution of the partners and case-studies.

3.4 Work-breakdown

The strong features of this project have been identified as including the fact that its technical soundness relies on the number of case-studies and that the future acceptance of the developed procedures relies on a large representative partnership.

It is clear that this project requires a definition phase. It therefore comprises two sequential work-packages:
- workpackage one : definition phase and limited feasibility demonstration of software certification. This phase will involve only a kernel of partners with a limited administrative over-head in terms of information flow.
- workpackage two : this phase will be the main project phase. it cannot be precisely defined yet, except in terms of general organization, tasks, and budgeting. The number of partners will slightly increase and it is anticipated that subcontracting will be used so as to incorporate efficiently such organizations as test-labs and software producers.

4. Conclusion and acknowledgments

Software certification is an appealing trend in today's software engineering world because it can greatly improve the overall quality level of software and help mastering the costs of software. Today, both certification methods must be considered and the resulting applicable certification techniques will clearly mix the two approaches.

It is clearly an aim of SCOPE to establish the correct ratio between the two as a function of the type of software to be certified and of the advances in product certification technology.

This paper is largely based on the technical presentation of SCOPE < SCOP-88 > which is a wide collective work. I am particularly grateful to B. Kitchenham and H.L. Hausen who have drafted the parts of the presentation on which this paper is based.

References

< HSEG > : HSE–Guidance of the Safe use of Programmable Electronic Systems.

< IEEE–83 > : ANSI/IEEE Std 729–1983, IEEE Standard Glossary of Software Engineering Terminology.

< RTCA–84 > : Software considerations in airborne systems and equipment certification. 1984.

< SCOP–88 > : Technical presentation of Esprit SCOPE project. Collective work by B. Kitchenham, O. Andersen, B. Cole, F. Copigneaux, C. Dale, W. Ehrenberger, H.L. Hausen, R. Hunter, B. Littlewood, M. Maiocchi.

3

THE ACCREDITATION PROCESS

JOHN A SLATER
Logica Consultancy Limited
64 Newman Street
London W1A 4SE

ABSTRACT

In the past users and developers have been frustrated by the lack of standards for products in the IT field. A significant obstacle to standardization has been the agreeing of the technical content of the standards. In some areas of IT applications these problems have been addressed and standards have been agreed and defined. IT business development would be greatly enabled if the emerging standards were underpinned by certification schemes. Certification schemes need to be developed to cover Quality Management Systems, IT products and personnel but if these are to be worthwhile they must be authoritative and have recognition abroad. Following the publication of Command 8621, Standards, Quality and International Competitiveness, UK Government criteria were defined to regulate certification bodies and the schemes they operate. This paper will review the current criteria and the work of the National Accreditation Council for Certification Bodies and how the existing procedures may be extended into the IT field.

INTRODUCTION

To gain a full appreciation of the accreditation process it is necessary to consider a number of related topics, these are:

- background

- formation of the NACCB (National Accreditation Council for Certification Bodies)

- role of the NACCB

- composition and structure of the NACCB

- criteria of competence used in accreditation

- the accreditation process.

BACKGROUND

There are three simple themes to keep in mind, these are:

- the accreditation mark

- the benefits to the purchaser

- to avoid reinventing the wheel.

The accreditation mark, see Figure 1, is essentially a mark of competence awarded by the Secretary of State for Trade and Industry on the recommendation of an impartial body, the NACCB. The mark is awarded to certification bodies who meet national criteria of competence.

Figure 1 The National accreditation mark

At the other end of the chain we have the purchaser of suppliers' products. Once a purchaser procures a software product or system and puts it into use the purchaser becomes dependent on the supplied items. The level of dependency varies according to the application but may include:

- corporate business performance

- operation of critical systems

- value added products or processes.

A simple example is the language compiler. The original supplier's dependency is about £150K, the approximate cost of the compiler's development. A modest sales target might be to 60 organizations who may in turn use the compiler on 20 projects. If each of these project developments is worth £80K the total development dependency is £96m. As indicated above it is the purchaser who has the real dependency once the end products of the compiler are operational and it is difficult to value this without knowledge of the application. However it will be a significant sum. Obviously there will be many other factors which affect the quality of the purchaser's system but given the total dependency issue the purchaser is interested in all aspects which can affect quality and should be interested in the compiler's ability to meet development needs and to generate good code. It is a common complaint amongst main suppliers that they have little visibility or evidence to offer to purchasers on software products supplied by subcontractors. Nevertheless the main supplier remains accountable in the first instance. The national accreditation mark may be transferred to a supplier, as a mark of competence and conformity, via a certification body who has been duly accredited by the NACCB. For products or services to receive this endorsement they must comply with the rules and procedures defined by the certification body's scheme.

FORMATION OF THE NACCB

In the UK Quality Management Standards and the National QA Framework have evolved over the last 25 years from principles and practices developed primarily for the engineering industry. [1] The main reports advocating a rational framework were:

- The Warner Report: 1977. Standards and Specifications in the Engineering Industries [2]

- CMND 8621: 1982. Standards, Quality and International Competitiveness [3]

- ACARD Report: 1982. Facing International Competition; The Impact on Product Designs of Standards, Regulations and Approvals [4]

When the Warner Report was initiated industry's industries' needs were perceived to be: the reduction of unit costs, improvement of quality, delivery within estimated timescales and a better export performance. Significant factors affecting the achievement of these goals were:

- the proliferation of procurement specifications and certification schemes for similar products

- the lack of standards relating to quality.

The principal recommendations which may be of interest to us were:

- for industry sectors to establish priorities for standards and specifications

- for purchasers, manufacturers and users to rationalize specifications and align UK and overseas requirements

- to ensure that the standards making machinery was adequate to meet the demands for effective standards

- for the building of a rational structure of quality assurance bodies with mutual acceptance of approvals to avoid multiple assessment

- to secure overseas acceptance of UK testing procedures

- to improve technical input into European standards making.

In July 1982 ACARD published their advisory report and in the same month the Government published CMD 8621 setting out the way ahead. These documents were complementary in that ACARD examined how standards, quality and regulatory systems of the UK's competitors influenced the international competitiveness of their manufacturing firms and CMO 8621 identified what changes were necessary in the UK to secure a similar advantage.

The main recommendations from ACARD were:

- that the benefits of Quality Management Systems based on BS 5750 [5] be published and that public and private purchasers make use of independent schemes for assessing supplier's quality procedures

- individual firms and trade associations establish more product certification and approval schemes particularly for internationally tradeable products where quality is important

- the government establishes a national accreditation scheme for certification and approval bodies; and that the Government should own, and retain control over the use of, a national mark of standing for quality.

CMND 8621 set out the Government's proposals for change and the main points were to:

- ensure standards reflect the requirements of world markets

- reduce the multiplicity of procurement specifications by relating requirements to standards

- establish a strong and coherent national standards making system

- devote extra effort and better resources to the development of relevant and clear standards

- promote harmonisation of standards within the European community

- encourage full participation by British experts in international standard work

- acknowledge that previous initiatives have not brought about widespread changes in attitudes

- encourage certification schemes

- introduce unified arrangements to accredit certification schemes

- require BSI, when producing new standards,to seek to ensure that these are suitable for regulatory, contract, certification and quality assurance purposes as appropriate

- promote a quality awareness campaign with emphasis on importance of education and training

- compile a register of quality assessed firms to BS 5750 or its direct equivalent.

It is against this background that the National Accreditation Council was brought into being in 1984 and for the first time a National QA framework began to emerge.

Having studied the main drivers for the establishment of the NACCB one may be tempted to ask if this history is relevant to software. It is my view that we need to avoid reinventing the wheel and if there is any doubt that this is happening here is a simple example concerning the basic definition of quality.

Quality

The totality of features and characteristics of a product or service that bear on its ability to satisfy stated or implied needs. ISO 8402: 1986

Software quality

The aggregate of all those attributes that, when possessed by software, will enable the software to perform its intended use. [P1061 Draft IEEE standard on software metrics]

One has to conclude that there is little effective difference between these two.

At present there is a great deal of concern about the safety and security implications of software based systems. If safety and security are required characteristics they thus become attributes of quality within the above definitions.

A recent ACARD report [6] on the software industry echoed much of what had been recorded before in regard to quality and certification. In particular, it was recommended that:

- a sustained and substantial UK software image enhancement programme be launched at home and abroad; part of this should be the establishment of a 'kite-mark' which indicates conformance to a high level of excellence

- a study into the issues of professional certification of software engineers, safety critical software and quality certification.

Aspects of these recommendations are currently being followed up by the IEE and the BCS.

ROLE OF THE NACCB

The NACCB was brought into being to provide a formal means of providing authoritative recognition of certification schemes. The main objectives are:

- enhance the authority and status of certification bodies

- encourage the development of new certification bodies

- facilitate the wider adoption of sound quality management systems and practices - by requiring BS 5750 : ISO 9000 or equivalent in criteria

- encourage the development of internationally harmonised accreditation criteria and to foster the growth of worldwide arrangements for reciprocal recognition of accredited certification bodies

- promote third party certification

- offer advice to the Government on certification.

To fulfilling these objectives the NACCB has brought together a national QA framework, see Figure 2.

At the top of the hierarchy is the NACCB which is a formally established body under the BSI's Royal Charter as an independent council. The NACCB undertakes, on behalf of the Secretary of State for Trade and Industry, the impartial assessment of certification bodies. For a certification body to become accredited it must satisfy national criteria covering integrity and technical competence. These criteria are based on harmonized international documentation covering the structure, operation and management of eertification bodies. Important features of the criteria require certification bodies to:

- be free of conflicting interests

- be staffed by competent, professional, managerial and technical staff

- have a governing board representative of the principal interests involved in certification.

Once accredited, a certification body may bear the Government's mark of accreditation.

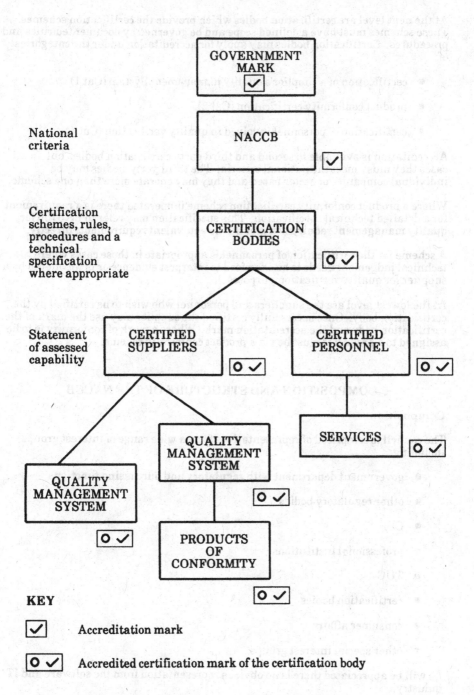

National
criteria

Certification
schemes, rules,
procedures and a
technical
specification
where appropriate

Statement
of assessed
capability

KEY

GOVERNMENT
MARK

NACCB

CERTIFICATION
BODIES

CERTIFIED
SUPPLIERS

CERTIFIED
PERSONNEL

SERVICES

QUALITY
MANAGEMENT
SYSTEM

QUALITY
MANAGEMENT
SYSTEM

PRODUCTS
OF
CONFORMITY

Accreditation mark

Accredited certification mark of the certification body

Figure 2. National QA Framework

At the next level are certification bodies which provide the certification schemes. These schemes must have a defined scope and be governed by documented rules and procedures. Certification bodies may apply for accreditation under the categories of:

- certification of a supplier's quality management System (Cat 1)

- product conformity certification (Cat 2)

- certification of personnel involved in quality verification (Cat 4).

Accreditation is available to second and third party certification bodies but in all cases they must meet the national criteria. The third party bodies may be individual companies or sector based and they may operate more than one scheme.

Where a product conformity certification scheme is operated there is a requirement for a detailed technical specification. This specification may refer to BS 5750 for quality management requirements or define equivalent requirements directly.

A scheme for the certification of personnel is appropriate in those cases where technical judgement needs to be exercised to interpret evidence or proof offered by a supplier for quality verification purposes.

At the lowest level are the suppliers and personnel who wish to be certified by the certification body. Once successfully certified the supplier may use the mark of the certification body and the accreditation mark. Where a mark of conformity is to be assigned to a product it must be via a product conformity scheme.

COMPOSITION AND STRUCTURE OF THE NACCB

Composition

The council is comprised of representatives from a wide range of interest groups including:

- government department with regulatory and purchasing functions

- other regulatory bodies

- CBI

- professional institutions

- TUC

- certification bodies

- consumer affairs

- other special interest groups.

As will be appreciated there is no obvious representation from the software and IT industry.

Structure

The overall structure of the NACCB is shown in figure 3.

The council is served by an accreditation unit, assessors and a number of specialist panels.

The accreditation unit coordinates and controls the accreditation scheme. Its main function is to ensure that the council's regulations and the national criteria are followed.

The assessment panel is responsible for recommending accreditation or otherwise of a certification body based on the evidence supplied by the accreditation unit and fieldwork by the NACCB assessors.

Where a certification body elects to use a quality management standard other than BS 5750 : ISO 9000, the equivalence panel is responsible for evaluating the alternative to ensure it is equivalent within the context of the application.

The appeals panel is responsible for advising the council on the merits or otherwise of an appeal from a certification body which fails to gain accreditation.

Ad hoc panels are conceived on an ' as and when ' basis to deal with specific issues which are outside the scope of interest of the other organizational functions.

CRITERIA OF COMPETENCE USED IN ACCREDITATION

The prime topics which form the criteria required by the Secretary of State for Trade and Industry and which must be complied with by a certification body are set out in Table 1.

Each topic has several requirements which are evaluated by the accreditation unit and the assessors when processing a certification body's application. Within an accreditation category all requirements must be satisfied in order to receive accreditation. For more information reference should be made to the NACCB documentation listed in Appendix 1.

The requirements are geared to ensure visibility of the constitution, management, operations and effectiveness of the certification body's schemes and to provide documentary evidence of this.

For the purposes of this paper, a synopsis of each element of the criteria is provided below.

Access

The services of the body shall be open to all and the governing procedures shall be administered in a non-discriminatory manner.

Administrative Structure

The body shall operate under a balanced governing board which has representation from those with an interest in certification. Permanent staff shall be responsible for the day to day operations and be free from control of those who may have a direct commercial interest in certification work.

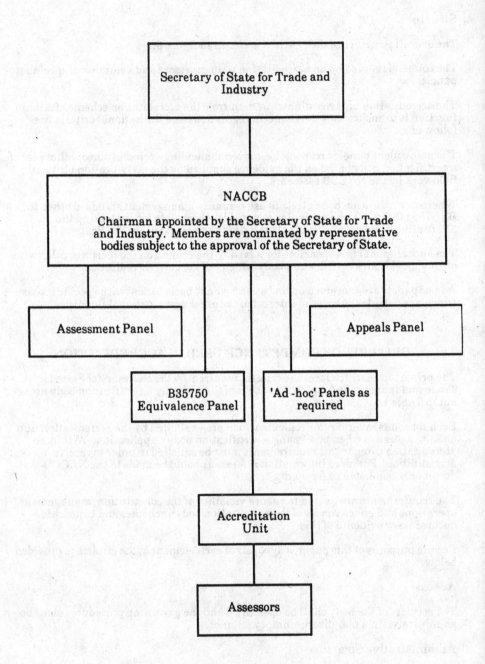

Figure 3. Overall Structure of the NACCB.

Terms of Reference

The governing board shall formulate certification policy, oversee policy implementation, oversee financial management and set up committees to undertake defined tasks as required.

Organizational Structure

The organizational structure shall show: management structure, financial arrangements, including rules and procedure, and the body's legal status.

Certification Staff

All staff shall be competent for the functions they undertake and up-to-date information on academic or other qualifications and experience shall be maintained. Staff shall have documented instructions pertaining to their duties and responsibilities.

If work is subcontracted, the certification body shall ensure that these staff meet the same qualifying requirements.

Where the certification body is concerned with personnel certification the staff shall be trained in the principles and practices of quality verification appropriate to the disciplines concerned.

Documentation and Change Control

Change control procedures shall be compatible with the requirements of BS 5750 particularly currency of documentation.

Records

Records shall be maintained to demonstrate how the certification procedures were applied. The records will be retained for a typical period of five years and be available to people judged to have an interest and right of access, whilst respecting confidentiality.

Supplier Quality Management Systems

The certification body shall require the applicant supplier to have a documented quality management system compliant with BS 5750, or equivalent; the appropriate parts being determined by the technical requirements under consideration. Where a technical specification is the source document, the certification body shall show that the quality management provisions are comparable with BS 5750.

Rules and Procedures for the Certification of Personnel

The certification body shall show, to the satisfaction of the Council, that its rules and procedures are sound and modern in terms of requirements for academic achievement, practice and experience. Wherever possible these shall be harmonized with appropriate national and international documentation.

Assessment Facilities Required

The certification body shall have the required resources in terms of facilities and staff to assess the applicants quality management system. For personnel certification the body shall have the resources necessary to appraise the applicant in line with the rules and procedures.

Surveillance of Suppliers

The certification body shall have the resources to ensure, by means of periodic inspection, that the suppliers' quality management systems continue to meet the requirements of BS 5750 or other equivalent standard. Where the body needs to confirm the suppliers' measurements competence, the resource used shall be accredited by NAMAS (National Measurement Accreditation Scheme).

Where surveillance is delegated, the certification body shall ensure all NACCB requirements are met.

The body will require the applicant supplier to keep a record of all complaints and remedial action. Statistics on these shall also be available to the Council.

Surveillance of Certificated Personnel

The certification body shall have the resources to ensure the continuing compliance of certificated personnel with its published rules and procedures. Requirements covering delegated surveillance, complaints and statistics are as previously stated.

Control Manual

The certification body shall have a control manual covering: legal structure, organization, staffing, training, details of procedures covering certification schemes, use of subcontractors and appeals.

Confidentiality

The certification body shall ensure the confidentiality of all activities in support of an application.

Publications

Up-to-date publications shall be available showing, as applicable: scope of qualified firms, certified products, certificated personnel and descriptions of the certification schemes.

Appeals

The certification body shall have established procedures for the consideration of appeals.

Misuse of Certificates or Marks of Conformity

The certification body shall exercise control on the use of its certificates of competence and marks of conformity. Incorrect references or misleading uses shall be followed up including legal action if necessary.

TABLE 1
NACCB criteria of competence requirements for certification

TOPIC	CAT 1 + 2	CAT 4
ACCESS	X	X
ADMINISTRATIVE STRUCTURE	X	X
GOVERNING BOARD TORs	X	X
ORGANISATIONAL STRUCTURES	X	X
CERTIFICATION STAFF	X	X
DOCUMENTATION AND CHANGE CONTROL	X	X
RECORDS	X	X
SUPPLIERS QUALITY MANAGEMENT SYSTEM	X	–
RULES OF PROCEDURE FOR CERTIFICATION OF PERSONNEL	–	X
ASSESSMENT FACILITIES	X	X
SURVEILLANCE OF SUPPLIERS	X	–
SURVEILLANCE OF CERTIFICATED PERSONNEL	–	X
CONTROL MANUAL	X	X
CONFIDENTIALITY	X	X
PUBLICATIONS	X	X
APPEALS	X	X
MISUSE OF A CERTIFICATE OF COMPETENCE	X	X
INTERNAL PERIODIC REVIEW	X	X
COMPLAINTS	X	X

Internal Periodic Review

The certification body shall undertake an internal periodic review of its activities for continuing compliance with NACCB criteria and the consistent application of its own procedures.

Complaints

The certification body shall keep a record of all complaints and follow up actions concerning its accredited activities.

THE ACCREDITATION PROCESS

The accreditation process starts by the certification body expressing interest in receiving the accreditation mark. The certification body then needs to assimilate all the relevant information and is provided with documentation explaining:

- NACCB prospectus
- regulations
- criteria
- guidelines on the compilation of a control manual
- product index guide
- application form.

This information is used by the certification body to caste their schemes into a form which will meet the national criteria. The criteria are general in nature and may be mapped to any discipline. However there are specific requirements in respect of BS 5750 and NAMAS. Recent work [7, 8] has confirmed that the quality management standard BS 5750 is applicable to software. NAMAS requirements would be applicable if traceable measurements were necessary.

Once the certification body has defined its operation and is satisfied it meets the national criteria, a formal application is made with a completed control manual.

The accreditation unit then undertakes a detailed examination of the documented procedures for compliance with the NACCB's regulations and criteria. Apart from the detailed work the unit needs to ensure that the category of certification applied for is consistent with the declared scope and that the scope itself is unambiguous. Any problems or non-compliances are then recorded and corrected.

Following this work the accreditation unit selects suitably qualified NACCB assessors who have experience within the same discipline area of the certification body. Once the assessors have been briefed on the work of the certification body and they have appraised the documentation a plan is drawn up for the on-site assessment activity. The object of the on-site work is to ensure that the scheme operated by the certification body is as defined in the control manual. In addition to visiting the certification body's HQ field visits will be made to suppliers to see how the practice of certification is conducted by the body's staff. The NACCB assessors need to consider the competence of the body's staff and how effective they were in evaluating the supplier's activities.

At each stage of the accreditation process reports are produced which record all the activities and findings of the accreditation unit and the assessors. When non-compliances have been rectified a report is passed to the assessment panel who then consider the findings and make an appropriate submission to the NACCB. If satisfied the council then recommends to the Secretary of State for Trade and Industry that the accreditation award be made.

Once a certification body is accredited it is subject to periodic confirmatory visits by the NACCB assessors to ensure standards are maintained.

FEASIBLE CERTIFICATION SCHEMES FOR SOFTWARE

At present, while there are certification bodies in the software and IT field, none, as yet, are accredited. Feasible certification schemes may be developed in the future covering:

(a) quality management systems

(b) product conformity against agreed sector specifications

(c) product conformity against a supplier's specification

(d) personnel certification for critical applications.

It is my view that schemes can be developed for (a), (b) and (d) without too much difficulty. However the standards and methods used to support the quality management system will need to be appropriate to the type of software and this must be reflected by the certification bodies scheme. Of interest to many suppliers particularly smaller companies ,will be schemes for products and systems against company specifications. The most cost effective schemes will be certification by suppliers' self declaration. The supplier will warrant the conformance of the product or system against his own specification. The certification scheme will ensure that the supply can provide evidence of quality management and continuing conformance to specification. If the certification body is accredited the products and systems may carry the authoritative accreditation mark. A major consideration for this type of scheme will be the level of disclosure and precision of the supplier's specification.

Certification of personnel for critical applications is likely to be more problematic due to:

● business practicalities

● the role of the purchaser.

If projects may only proceed with the continuing presence of a certified person, difficulties will arise if this person becomes unavailable or changes jobs. Where a purchaser, due to procurement practice, can have an effect on product quality the purchasers will also need to employ certified personnel.

SUMMARY

Whilst the national QA framework has evolved without any particular regard for the software and IT industry it is nevertheless applicable. What is needed now is for the industry to decide what types of certification schemes are of benefit, and for professional bodies and staff to come forward and strengthen the framework. The NACCB criteria are based on harmonized international documentation and work is in hand for mutual recognition of accreditation marks. If adopted the standing of the UK industry will be enhanced aboard and an enabling mechanism would be in place to improve quality.

REFERENCES

1   Slater, J A, Trends in Quality Assurance. Journal of the Institute of Quality Assurance, September 1988.

2   Warner, F, The Warner Report: Standards and Specifications in the Engineering Industries, 1977.

3   CMND 8621, Standards, Quality and International Competitiveness, HMSO 1982.

4   ACARD Report, Facing International Competition; The Impact on Products Designs of Standards, Regulations, Certification and Approvals, HMSO 1982.

5   BS 5750, 1979 British Standards Institute, 2 Park Street, London W1A 2BS.

6   ACARD Report, Software; A Vital Key to UK Competitiveness 1986.

7   Logica Report, Quality Management Standards for Software, Dept Trade and Industry, 67-74 Victoria Street, London SW1E 6SW 1988.

8   Price Waterhouse Report, Software Quality Standards. The Cost, and the Benefits. Dept of Trade and Industry, 67-74 Victoria Street, London SW1E 6SW, 1988.

APPENDIX 1

KEY NACCB DOCUMENTS

1   Regulations.

2   Criteria of Competence

   (a) Certification of suppliers
        Quality management systems (Cat 1)

   (b) Product conformity certification (Cat 1).

3   Criteria of competence

   (a) Certification of personnel engaged in quality verification.

4   Criteria to be met by NACCB assessors.

5   Regulations governing the use of the accreditation mark.

6   Guidelines on the compilation of a control manual for certification bodies.

7   Application form.

8   Directory of accredited certification bodies.

4

MILITARY STANDARDS AND SOFTWARE CERTIFICATION

K Geary BSc, C.Eng, MBCS, GIMA
Sea Systems Controllerate
Ministry of Defence
Foxhill
Bath BA1 5AB

ABSTRACT

Software now being used for control of equipment that has the potential to endanger life or limb must be developed to rigorous standards. This paper discusses certification requirements of existing standards and the new Draft MOD Policy for the development of Safety Critical Software. These new requirements, which will be defined in more detail in the proposed Interim Defence Standard 00-55, lay down a number of measures to be taken during software development leading to certification of the end product. A possible approach aimed at giving the customer visibility and confidence in the correct application of these measures is outlined.

Caveat

This paper reflects on the contents of the Draft MOD Policy for Safety Critical Software [1] which is in circulation to Industry for comment at the time of writing. Being a draft, the requirements and terminology of the Policy statement may be subject to change. The views expressed in this paper are those of the author and do not necessarily represent those of the Department.

INTRODUCTION

The use of software for the control of equipment such as aircraft or missile flight control surfaces, weapons systems firing arcs and nuclear reactor protection has given rise to concern over the integrity (or "reliability") of such software [2][3]. There is wide recognition that it is very difficult, if not impossible, to guarantee error-free software. A number of methodologies and practices have become available and may be used, in addition to well established software engineering practices, to achieve a high level of software integrity in order to minimise risks to safety. The application of these techniques is considered in the context of their contribution to the process of software certification.

The paper is divided into 3 main areas of discussion. Initially, current standards and practices involved in software certification are discussed. The current draft of the MOD Policy Statement on Safety Critical Software is examined with respect to its requirements for software certification. Finally, proposals are put forward on providing MOD with visibility and assurance that safety critical software development and certification are being carried out in accordance with requirements. The conclusions highlight the variation in meaning of the term "software certification" and the change of responsibility for certification arising from the new draft MOD Policy.

DISCUSSION

Software Categories

Three basic software categories are considered, namely "ordinary", high integrity and safety critical software. In terms of the design aim to attain compliance with the functional requirement, there is no difference between these categories. The difference lies in the possible consequence of malfunction and thereby the incentive to commit greater resources to ensuring that the software is correct. The more serious the effect of malfunction, the greater the commitment to attaining correct functionality, or greater "reliability". Where there is an impact on safety, there may be a requirement for certification of the application software to convey confidence to the customer that the software comes up to some form of standard. Yet, a customer would not wish to accept erroneous software, even in the "ordinary" category. There is, therefore, on reason why the concept of certification should be confined to safety related software.

Software Reliability

The issue of reliability should be considered by the customer from a systems viewpoint, since both software and hardware design will affect this aspect. Most hardware failures are due to wear-out; hardware design errors are rarely if ever included in reliability calculations. However all software errors are specification and design errors and therefore not time dependent. Software does not degrade with use and, being purely a design specification, has no tangible existence beyond the hardware on which it is held. Software faults only manifest themselves when stimulated by particular combinations of input data. For example, software in a military system may function perfectly in peacetime but fail on transition to exercise or war conditions.

In such cases, the software fails to perform as expected resulting in the system failing to carry out the task in hand. The fault may be attributable to an error in the coding, the design or, more likely, the software specification. It will probably have laid undiscovered since system acceptance and only manifested itself when triggered by a new combination of input data. The occurrence of software failures is related more to change of operational circumstances than to the wear and tear arising from use and the passage of time.

Current Position

There are a number of standards currently available which are based largely on conventional software engineering. A review of these standards reveals that "certification" is mainly confined to the concept of registration of a company's practices and procedures as being compliant with a quality assurance standard. Inspection of procedures and their application can be a relatively infrequent sampling audit. In the case of MOD contractor assessment, there can be as much as 3 years between audits. More frequent monitoring, by MOD, of quality control on a project basis is provided by a quality assurance representative who monitors compliance with the quality plan.

Ordinary Software

The MOD uses AQAP-1 [4] as the general requirement standard for quality assurance. AQAP-13 [5] provides a similar requirement directed at software. An audit is carried out every 2 to 3 years and, following a successful audit, the company is re-registered for a further period of 2 years. If the company requests audit for compliance with AQAP-13, software practices are audited at the same time as the AQAP-1 audit is carried out. A favourable audit result against AQAP-13 will be acknowledged by letter as there is no formal registration mechanism for this standard.

Recently, BS5750 [6] has been supported by a schedule which addresses software quality assurance. There is an audit and registration process carried out by the British Standards Institute (BSI). It is also common for some large companies to assess subcontractors to BS5750 as an aid to their own quality procedures. However, it should be noted that anyone can assess a firm to BS5750, but only the BSI can register that firm after carrying out its own assessment.

A feature of the BS5750 software quality schedule is the provision for the customer to request a certificate of conformancy from the supplier. This certificate is the supplier's own declaration that the software for a project has been developed in accordance with procedures registered to BS5750. The certificate of conformancy is a useful and progressive step towards self certification by the software developer. However, there has been some suggestion that the reqirement for this certificate should be removed from BS5750. One would not anticipate that a conscientious quality minded software developer would object to self certification. Discontinuation of the certificate of conformancy would, therefore, be a step backwards in terms of responsible quality control management.

The customer usually relies on equipment acceptance trials for establishing compliance with the specification. Acceptance trails are a test of the system as a whole and, as such, will only exercise a minute proportion of the software. Apart from the signature of a quality representative on the delivery note, there is no evidence required of compliance with quality procedures or compliance with the specification. The customer project manager's signature on the delivery note is in effect a certification of satisfaction with the system and, by implication, satisfaction with the software.

High Integrity

High integrity software is software for which it is essential that there are no errors. Such software would probably be controlling a system which must meet stringent reliability requirements. Safety may not be a factor but design and development practices for "ordinary" software would not be sufficient to give confidence that the software is of adequate reliability to prevent a degradation of system performance.

A high integrity annex, included in NES620 [7] since 1986, defines procedures and practices, additional to Defence Standard 00-16 [8] which addresses "ordinary" software. If the software is classed as high integrity, the software developer is required to justify non-use of any of the listed techniques which will not be applied. No specific certification is required but there is a clause requiring access to the software, including all documentation, by the customer representatives. This makes provision for MOD to arrange for any additional or independent validation and verification thought necessary in support of acceptance.

US military standards refer to software as "mission critical". This leaves the level software integrity or reliability to be interpreted in relation to the importance of the mission or operational task, which could be any category. MIL Standards 2167A and 2168 [9][10] rely very much on independent validation and verification (IV&V) of the software, although the requirements concentrate on verification. An IV&V team, from a different company under a different contract to the customer, is required to test and evaluate the application software. This team's report provides the evidence, and implied certification, that the software meets its specification.

Safety Critical

With safety critical software, a malfunction could cause risk to human life. Software in this category is a class of high integrity software where reliability is of the utmost importance if a high standard of safety is to be attained. Recent standards dealing with safety critical software tend to assume that conventional good software engineering practices are applied and concentrate on additional techniques.

Well known in the air world is RTCA DO-178A [11], and its derivatives. This standard aims to describe techniques and methods that may be used for the orderly development and management of software for airborne computer based equipment. The declaration in its scope states that it is only a guide that may be used in support of certification programmes. Although it is written in terms of conventional software engineering of 3 years ago, it was made sufficiently flexible to enable interpretation to include alternative and future standards and procedures. Certification is defined as obtaining regulatory agency approval that the equipment complies with all applicable government regulations. Existence and knowledge of applicable government regulations is assumed, for example, in reference to the Certification Plan which is only described by a brief list of attributes.

Interim Defence Standard 00-31 [12] provides an interpretation of DO-178A, setting out the techniques and methods required for the development of software for MOD high integrity airborne applications. The contractor is required to prepare and submit a cerification plan for approval to the regulatory authority designated by the MOD project director. Certification of the software is defined as formal acceptance by the MOD project director that the software is suitable for service use in its intended system. In this case certification is limited to the system, making it necessary for the software to be recertified if applied to a different system. Design certification is carried out at system level in accordance with Defence Standard 05-123 [13].

The high integrity software requirements in NES620 address safety critical software [14]. Requirements specifically include the use of formal mathematical specifications and formal validation of the coding. These requirements are expressed in more detail in Ordnance Board Procedures 42413 and 42393 [15][16]. Both the Naval and the Ordnance Board standards require a satisfactory validation and verification report to provide the evidence that the software meets its specification.

The US Department of Defense have issued MIL STD 882B [17]. The requirements of this standard specify rigorous procedural management and independent validation and verification of the

software in line with MIL STD 2168. The author has seen little
evidence of application of MIL STD 882B to military projects and
recent verbal reports suggest that the requirements have been
found to be too bureaucratic.

New MOD Requirements

Experience has shown that guides have little contractual
significance. Competitive tendering for fixed price contracts
encourages economies which rightly concentrate on compliance with
mandatory requirements. Areas which are only covered by guidance
can be subject to varying interpretation making. intended
requirements difficult to enforce. The engineering opinions of
safety assessors, who are only concerned with system safety, may
differ from those of contractors who must also strike a balance
with very relevant commercial aspects such as cost and
timescales.

In order to ensure that required practices and procedures
are applied, MOD is drafting a Safety Critical Software Policy
and supporting Interim Defence Standard 00-55 which will lay down
requirements that are mandatory. These requirements include the
accumulation of documentary evidence, demonstrating compliance
with obligatory techniques, leading to certification, by the
Design Authority, of conformance with the Standard.

Applicability

One of the most important considerations from the outset, in
any project, is to decide whether any of the software will be
safety critical. In order to ensure that all applicable software
is specified and developed using the required procedures, the
draft policy requires that all software should be regarded as
safety critical until a hazard analysis is carried out. This
requirement acts as a catch all, making it necessary to show that
software is not safety critical before the policy and Interim
Defence Standard 00-55 cease to become applicable.

Effectively, the certification process starts here. A signed
statement that an item of software is not safety critical is
itself a certificate, whereas a hazard analysis report,
identifiying safety critical software, will form the first part
of the evidence to be compiled in support of safety
certification. The requirement applies not only at project
initiation but also throughout the whole lifecycle. Design
modifications must be considered for impact on safety.

Responsibilities

It is important to clearly define the responsibilities of
all parties. The MOD project manager is the Software Safety
Authority and, as such, must be satisfied that the Design

Authority activities are compliant with requirements. The Design Authority is responsible for the management of software safety, and the appointment of an independent software safety assessor.

The appointment of an independent software safety assessor should not be seen as relieving the Design Authority of its obligations to ensure rigorous compliance with the requirements of Interim Defence Standard 00-55. Placement of responsibility is seen as a major incentive for all concerned to avoid any temptation to place a higher priority on commercial or other aspects not connected with safety, to the possible detriment of the provisions of the standard.

Safety Assurance

Like quality assurance, safety assurance is obtained through documented procedures and records. Procedures to be followed are laid down in the software safety plan, which defines the special measures required for the development of safety critical software. These measures are extra to normal conventional software engineering quality control which must also be applied.

It is essential that the software safety plan be drawn up and agreed by all concerned prior to commencement of software development. If the software safety plan is not formally issued at the start, any development carried out prior to its issue is unlikely to be classified as compliant because that work will have been performed without the benefit of formal procedures or the necessary evidence to support safety certification.

The safety record book should contain a detailed audit trail of actions completed in accordance with the software safety plan. It provides the evidence that the plan has been correctly followed and that all activities have been executed to the satisfaction of the Design Authority and the independent software safety assessor.

Software Assessor

The independent software safety assessor provides independent monitoring of the software development to ensure the software safety plan has been implemented and correctly carried out. This assessor must be managerially independent of the software development personnel. The assessor, like the development personnel, must also be adequately trained and qualified for the assessment role. This means that the assessor must have a sound knowledge of the methods and tools used for the development of safety critical software, and have visibility of how and when they were applied on on the project.

Managerial independence implies the independent software safety assessor should be from a separate organisation such as an independent contractor. However, it may be permissible for large defence contractors to use an independent software safety assessor from a different site within their own organisations. It is unclear at this stage whether an assessor from the same organisation would be acceptable. The contractor would need to demonstrate independence could be upheld and would need to convince the MOD project manager and appropriate MOD safety authority that the assessor will be free from any corporate pressures that might pejudice judgement.

Methods and Tools

Emphasis is placed on mathematically based methods and tools aimed at achieving software that is as fault free as possible. The requirement is that the text based engineering specification for the software must be expressed in a formal mathematical notation which should also be used to express design. The software must then be coded using a rigorously defined high level language, or subset of a high level language, and compiled using only a compiler that is covered by a language validation certificate. To assist with static analysis of the code, formal mathematical assertions from the specification and design need to be embedded in the code. Static analysis of the code [18] is then to be carried out, complemented by dynamic analysis using a test coverage monitor [19].

When the aim is to achieve very high integrity software, it may appear intuitively that more testing is all that should be applied. Extensive independent testing is a useful and necessary technique, identified in the draft policy as dynamic analysis, which should be included in the range of measures applied. However its limitations should be recognised. The input domain, even for a small program, will almost certainly be too large to test exhaustively. For example, with only four bytes of information the input domain is in the order of 4000 million possibilities. Dynamic analysis should emulate, as far as practical, the unpredictable nature of the operational environment while exercising every statement and every branch decision at least once. It is important to test at the boundaries of the input domain and to cover a representative sample of any physically feasible inputs outside the expected domain.

Insistence on the use of formal mathematically based methods and tools reflects the need to add rigor to software development [20]. Formal mathematical notation can now be used to precisely express specifications and design. There is, at present, no policy to use a single formal mathematical notation although it is likely that MOD will adopt a preferred notation in time. Notations receiving most attention in the UK are 'Z' and VDM [21][22]. In addition, mathematically based software static analysis tools are available [23][24]. These tools enable detailed analysis of the design and code which can be used to identify logic errors that may cause the program to malfunction.

Certification

In the absence of appropriate standards, some software developers have relied on the application of traditional software engineering practices to reflect their best endeavours to produce high integrity software. This has subsequently posed a problem at acceptance where a safety assessment authority has been required to certify a system as safe when it has insufficient evidence that the controlling software is correct. Thus, the intention is that the draft policy and standard will lay down mandatory requirements based on the methodologies and tools which are acknowledged to benefit software safety and integrity. Procedures are necessary to ensure the application of these requirements.

It is essential to adhere rigorously to the safety plan. Unauthorised or unintended deviation could be viewed by safety assessors as compromising safety procedures, which may create problems at certification. The safety record book or log provides the documentary evidence that safety assurance activities have been carried out. It should provide an audit trail which may be inspected and verified by safety assessors. Both the safety plan and the safety record book are central to the rigorous procedures required in support of safety assurance. They specify and record the application of the tools and methods required by the policy.

The certificate of conformance with Interim Defence Standard 00-55 should be signed by the Design Authority and the independent software safety assessor. This certificate is backed by the documentary evidence provided by the software safety plan, the safety record log book and supporting documentation. Acceptance will then be based on normal procedures and trials plus the certificate of conformance and its supporting evidence. All must be to the satisfaction of the MOD project manager and safety assurance authority.

Visibility

The MOD project manager and the MOD safety assurance bodies will wish to be assured that safety management has been properly planned and is being carried out in accordance with the agreed safety plan. Monitoring of correct application of techniques would follow the development cycle phases, as is current practice for progress monitoring. However there are 3 key milestones at which the safety assurance authority should formally agree that requirements and their application are satisfactory.

The first milestone is tender preparation within MOD. Under the draft MOD Policy the likelihood of safety critical software being embedded in the required system must be identified. If safety critical software is likely, the MOD project manager must ensure that contract requirements are adequate. The next milestone is bid assessment where the safety authorities will wish to be assured that the successful bidder has identified any safety critical software resulting from system design and bid proposals are fully compliant with safety management requirements. The final key milestone is at certification and acceptance where assurance of compliance with the safety plan will be required.

Questionnaire

In order to assist the correct presentation of safety assurance justifications, a safety critical software development questionnaire is being devised for use with Naval weapons systems. The questionnaire is divided into 3 parts in line with the 3 key milestones. Part 1 should be completed by the MOD project manager prior to invitation to tender. It asks whether the system is likely to contain embedded safety critical software and, if so, whether the appropriate requirements have been included in the tender invitation.

Part 2 of the questionnaire, which should be completed by the bidder for each tender return, asks for information necessary to establish compliance of safety management procedures proposed by each bidder. After award of contract and completion of software development, or maintenance and modification in the in-service phase, part 3 should be completed by the design authority. This part requests evidence of compliance with the safety plan and, when signed by the design authority and the independent software safety assessor, would suit as a certificate that software conforms to safety requirements.

Environment Certification

The development environment is the key to ensuring software is produced to a satisfactory level of integrity. As outlined above, environment certification only extends to audit and registration of quality control procedures. Some regulatory bodies inspect and register safety management practices of system manufacturers in a similar fashion, and it is possible that, in time, MOD may likewise assess and register safety practices. However, assessment and registration of procedures omits two other important aspects which contribute to software safety.

Personnel are arguably the most important factor in providing a good software development environment. Procedures and tools cannot compensate for a thorough understanding of the likely problems and the need to take a professional approach to the task. A full appreciation of the reasons behind the need for safety procedures is a powerful motivation to work within those procedures.

The second aspect, sometimes forgotten when assessing quality procedures, is the quality of tools. Most software developers apply tests to a newly delivered or updated tool before it is applied to software development. However, a large program cannot reasonably be tested beyond the practical limits of acceptance trials. One cannot "calibrate" a software tool in the same way as generalised quality assurance standards require machinery production and inspection tools to be calibrated. To be reasonably confident that a tool is of adequate quality, the user needs to know something about the way the tool was developed.

Certification Limits

The existence of a certificate for an item of software does not necessarily imply that the software is cleared for use in all circumstances. It must not be forgotten that systems and any embedded software are produced to conform to a specification. That specification should lay down the scenario within which the software is required to operate. Subsequent certification will therefore apply to the software for the functions and operational environment described in the specification. Consequently that certification becomes invalid when the software is used in a system or for a task which was not covered by the specification.

Interim Defence Standard 00-31 recognises these potential problems, arising from alternative use of software, in its definition of certification which ties software to use in the system for which it was designed. One of the problems that can be experienced is that users become so confident in the performance of a software based system that they stretch its operation beyond the limits of the functional specification. Under these circumstances the software may not perform as expected, possibly resulting in an accident.

CONCLUSIONS

The term "software certification" may be interpreted in several ways. Firstly there is the well known certificate of registration of software quality assurance procedures. Compilers for Ada, Pascal an CORAL 66 may be validated and certified as compliant with their language standards. Software personnel who are graduates are given a certificate showing satisfactory attainment of a qualification. Although qualifications of personnel tend to receive little attention, personnel are the most crucial element of any software development environment.

There has been debate about some form of certification for software tools. Assessing compliancy with specifications contained in sales literature has been considered, but so far assessment in this area has been confined to evaluation. With the exception of compilers, few tool specifications are the same and unless there is a generic specification, evaluation is the only practical course. However, it would be possible, and even desirable, to require registration of quality assurance of the development procedures for tools, which should be sold with a certificate of compliancy or a BSI kite mark.

Bespoke application software has traditionally been certified by the customer in the form of formal acceptance. The US approach of independent validation and verification has not been taken up on a significant scale in the UK and, where it has been tried, there have sometimes been problems associated with design disclosure. With the BS5750 certificate of conformancy and the requirement in the new draft MOD Policy for design authority to provide similar certification for safety critical software, we are beginning to see a shift of responsibility for certification. This shift relieves the customer of the traditional responsibility of providing quality or safety assurance and places that responsibility with the contractor who controls work practices and compliance with standards.

Copyright (C) Controller HMSO London 1988.

REFERENCES

1. Ministry of Defence, Draft MOD Policy Statement for the Procurement and use of Software for Safety Critical Applications, D/DPP/5/1/11/2, 25 April 1988.

2. ACARD, "Software - A vital key to UK comptitiveness" HMSO, London 1986.

3. Thomas M., The British Computer Society Annual Lecture, "Should We Trust Computer Systems?", Praxis Systems plc, 1988.

4. NATO, Allied Quality Assurance Procedure 1, "NATO Requirements for an Industrial Quality Control System", Military Agency for Standardisation, 1981.

5. NATO, Allied Quality Assurance Procedure 13, "NATO Software Quality Control System Requirements", Military Agency for Standardisation, 1981.

6. BS5750 "Quality Systems", British Standards Institute

7. Ministry of Defence, Naval Engineering Standard 620 "Requirements for Software for use with Digital Processors", issue 3, MOD Controllerate of the Navy, 1986.

8. Ministry of Defence, Defence Standard 00-16 "Guide to the Achievement of Quality in Software", issue 1, Directorate of Standardization, Glasgow, 1984.

9. MIL STD 2167A "Defense System Software Development", US Department of Defense, 1988.

10. MIL STD 2168 "Software Quality Evaluation", US Department of Defense

11.   Radio   Technical   Commission   for   Aeronautics,   DO-178A "Software Considerations in Airborne Systems and   Equipment Certification", RTCA 1985.

12.   Ministry of Defence, Interim Defence Standard 00-31 "The Development of Safety Critical Software for Airborne Systems", issue 1, Directorate of Standardization, Glasgow, 1987.

13.   Ministry of Defence, Defence Standard 05-123 "Technical Procedures for the Procurement of Aircraft, Weapon and Electronic Systems", Directorate of Standarization, Glasgow.

14.   Geary K.,   Beyond Good Practices - A Standard for Safety Critical Software, "Achieving Safety and Relibility with Computer Systems", Elsevier Applied Science, London, 1987, pp.232-241.

15. Ministry of Defence, OB PROC 42413 "Principles of Design and Use for Electrical Circuits Incorporating Explosive Components", Unpublished Ministry of Defence Ordnance Board Report.

16. Ministry of Defence, OB PROC 42393 "The Assessment of Safety Critical Software Applications in Weapons Systems", Unpublished Ministry of Defence Ordnance Board Report.

17. MIL STD 882B "Military Standard System Safety Program Requirements", US Department of Defense.

18.   Phillips B.P. & Howe S.G., Verification - the Practical Problems,   "Achieving   Safety and Relibility with   Computer Systems", Elsevier Applied Science, London, 1987, 89-99.

19.   Bishop P.G.L., et seq., STEM - A Project on Software Test and Evaluation Methods, "Achieving Safety and Relibility with Computer Systems", Elsevier Applied Science, London, 1987, 100-117.

20.   Hoare A., Maths Adds Safety to Computer Programs, New Scientist, 18 Sept 1986, pp.53-56.

21. STARTS, "VDM - A Debrief Report", National Computing Centre.

22. STARTS, "Z - A Debrief Report", National Computing Centre.

23.   Clutterbuck D.L. and Carre B.A., The Verification of Low-Level Code, Software Engineering Journal, May 1988, pp.97-111.

24. Webb J.T. & Mannering D., Verification of a Safety Critical System, "Achieving Safety and Relibility with   Computer Systems", Elsevier Applied Science, London, 1987, pp.44-58.

5

THE ASSESSMENT OF SAFETY RELATED SYSTEMS CONTAINING SOFTWARE

P.J.NEILAN
Manager Navaids Software
National Air Traffic Services
45-59 Kingsway, London WC2B 6TE

ABSTRACT

This paper provides a summary of the experiences of the
National Air Traffic Services in the assessment and approval
of ground-based navigational aids for aircraft when embedded
software is used in the design. The paper describes how
having established the problems related to software and its
consequences for assessment, NATS is evolving a strategy for
the future. The evaluation of modern tools and techniques in
real projects is also described and conclusions drawn.

INTRODUCTION

NATS is a joint Civil Aviation Authority - Ministry of
Defence organisation responsible for the provision of the UK
Air Traffic Control and air navigation services both en
route, and at those airports where NATS provides ATS. The
services provided include the operation of air traffic
control and facilities and supporting ATC infrastructure
including: Communications, Radar, Navigational aids for en-
route and landing guidance and ATC information systems. NATS
specifies, procures, installs, commissions and approves these
systems.

Types of Systems

This paper is mainly concerned with the ground-based navaids
which are used to guide the aircraft along the airways -VOR
and DME, and through airport approach and landing - ILS, MLS.
Bearing and range information is provided by VOR and DME
respectively to the pilot and ILS provides approach guidance
at a fixed glide angle to the extended centre-line of the
runway to touch-down and along the runway. The instrument
landing system, ILS is classified into three categories (Cat
1, 2 and 3) according to its operational use. Reliability and
integrity requirements are based on this classification. A

Cat 3 ILS, which may be operated in conditions of very low
visibility and no decision height, must meet the most
stringent requirements. Amongst other things these specify
that a potentially hazardous loss-of-integrity during any one
landing (i.e. a period of about 30 seconds) should occur
with a frequency of less than 0.5×10^{-9}.

System Architecture
A typical navaid consists of an antenna array fed from
transmitters which generates the RF power and guidance
signals. Three levels of automatic monitoring are usually
employed - internal (within the equipment), integral (within
the antenna) and external (off-air via a separate antenna).
The primary functions monitored include the guidance signal
and the signal level and should errors in these parameters
exceed preset limits the system is shut down via a control
unit. To ensure availability, a complete standby system is
usually provided which is immediately and automatically
brought into service when required. Dual monitors are
operated with each transmitter and each monitor may have
redundancy in the more critical channels. An integrity
failure is deemed to have occurred when a transmitter is
radiating erroneous guidance outside the limits set and the
monitor fails to recognise it or the control unit fails to
switch the faulty transmitter off.

ICAO
NATS specifications are designed to meet the requirements of
the International Civil Aviation Organisation-ICAO which sets
standards and recommended practices-SARPS for aviation
procedures and equipment, including ground-based navaids.
ICAO, which is a specialised agency within the UN and has 140
member States, sets up panels of experts to study and make
recommendations on the technical and operational requirements
relating to air navigation services on facilities. The All
Weather Operations Panel is one such panel and it is
currently completing the specification for the new microwave
landing system MLS, which is to replace ILS by the year 2000.
The Air Navigation Council of ICAO ratifies and disseminates
the work of the panel from its headquarters in Montreal. ICAO
specifications are unique in so much as they achieve almost
worldwide acceptance in the aviation community because the
uniform application of these specifications is important to
ensure compatibility and inter-operability between the
systems and services operated by each state.

Systems Approval
Generally speaking, systems are approved by NATS following
extensive factory and field tests, analysis and acceptance
testing against the requirements specification. They are
accepted into service following successful commissioning
which for ground based navaids also includes flight
calibration. The permitted category of operation however, may
depend upon further evidence gained over time. With ILS for
example, a new system would not be permitted into full
category 3 service until it had demonstrated appropriate
reliability, typically an MTBF of 4000 hours to 95%

confidence. A certificate is issued to the aerodrome operator for the category of operation for which the system qualifies. Issue of the certificate is a NATS HQ function.There are broadly three areas of interest for assessment:

1. Those systems which are designed and built specifically to NATS requirements.

2. Proprietary systems available off the shelf and offered to meet NATS requirements.

3. Proprietary systems offered for approval by NATS for use in the UK, but not being purchased by NATS for its own use.

For these systems NATS will want assurance that the operational, system and safety objectives have been correctly and completely captured by the contractor and implemented in the design; that the product is maintainable and that the tools personnel and maintenance procedures are available to do this.

System integrity

The traditional approach to defining the integrity requirements has been to calculate the failure rates for the system functions using the MIL Handbook 217(e) and to use these in conjunction with a hazard analysis to arrive at a figure for integrity. The use of self tests, monitoring and maintenance intervals are also an important consideration.The final system invariable includes some form of redundancy to achieve the required level of availability.

It is currently not possible to predict accurately the failure rates for software and so the traditional approach is no longer appropriate, as the risk cannot be quantified. NATS has to assess whether the system requirement has been met and to do this we need to know how the system works and how it came into existence- and this task is also made more difficult by involving software in the design.

PAST EXPERIENCE

Over the last six years we have gained some experience of the problems in assessing systems containing software. As a rule the task of analysing the software has been carried out by external bodies on behalf of NATS or by the contractors themselves using a number of tools, including the static analysers MALPAS and SPADE and various computer utilities. Difficulties have arisen not just because the systems contained software but because the particular implementations did not lend themselves to analysis. Attempting to verify that the software was an implementation of the specification was often unfeasible resulting from the unnecessary complexity of the software coupled with inadequate design documentation. To counter this, static analysis tools were used to extract a "specification" from the code.By referring this "specification" back to the designer significant design errors could be revealed. As a consequence NATS found itself involved in necessarily extensive and costly design approval activity and in some cases was unable to approve systems as offered for use in the UK.

Lessons Learned.
A number of lessons can be learned from these and other systems which have been reviewed and there is nothing new here for those attending this forum.

1. Retrospective analysis-or so-called reverse engineering can prove impossible to carry out and will certainly be very expensive.

2. Producing documentation early in the development life cycle obviates the need to derive final system documentation through reverse engineering.

3. The documentation should be produced to such a level as to make the design visible to engineers and management alike, allowing for an effective implementation of control and monitoring of the development process. Examples of visible design include data flow diagrams, structure diagrams, pseudo code, design skeletons and data dictionaries and software design descriptions.

4. A well controlled and documented design provides the customer with a measure of protection against the effects of staff changes (both customer and supplier) or even against the demise of the supplying company.

5. A development methodology must be specifically agreed in advance, addressing the requirements for design documentation, design reviews, testing etc if there is to be any prospect of validating the complete system.

6. A need exists for the alignment of 'standards' at an international level in order that proprietary systems using computer-based technology can be considered safe for use in the UK and elsewhere, and to avoid the commercial embarrassment arising from the rejection by Authorities of developed systems. This was also a theme in the ACARD report[7].

7. Finally, and perhaps the most important thing of all, it is necessary to have the right people with the appropriate depth of knowledge and skill and the management and tool support to do the job.

RESPONSE TO THE PROBLEM

It was clear that if software was to be acceptable for use in safety related systems then the task had to be tackled from the beginning. A special Section was set up within the Directorate responsible for Navaids to study and evaluate the

available tools and techniques and to develop a strategy for
dealing with the problem. The task has been made a little
easier by the significant increase in awareness of the issues
in the UK, thanks to forums such as this. There is broad
agreement on the problem and much agreement on how to tackle
it. There is less progress in the application of the new
methods and case studies are hard to come by.

In developing the specification of the new MLS, ICAO
also became concerned about the impact of software on the
integrity of the system. A special working group was set up
in 1987 to develop a set of guide-lines for using software in
MLS which would be acceptable to all member States. The group
was made up of members from USA, Canada, France, Germany and
the UK. A number of papers were prepared on behalf of the
NATS member of this group and these are noted in the
references. The guide-lines are in an advanced state of
development and the group is now responding to concern
expressed about the lack of experience in applying these
techniques.
Some key points from these ICAO MLS guide-lines are:

1.   Software can only have design errors, and as it is not
     possible to predict these no quantitative assessment of
     the risk associated with software can be given.

2.   The system design must be such as to minimise the effect
     on the system integrity of any errors in the software.

3.   Confidence in the software must be based on the extent
     to which its behaviour can be established by logical
     reasoning.To make this possible the design and
     development must be performed in a certain way.

4.   The development must be a top-down process with
     documentation produced as an integral part of this
     process. At each stage of the development there should
     be consistency checking from level to level supported by
     trusted software tools.

5.   The programming should be performed in a single high-
     order language or,if necessary a safe subset of this.

6.   Software testing must be performed in accordance with a
     carefully developed test plan.

     The guide-lines also address the quality of
documentation, the need for configuration management,
independent verification and validation and software
maintenance.NATS basic strategy will be underpined by the
material developed for ICAO with due regard to DO 178A, AQAP
1 and 13, the STARTS guide and the new DEF Stan 0055 [3, 4,
5, 6.] In support of this we have endeavoured to apply and
evaluate the new methods through some small but non safety-
critical embedded systems being developed for NATS.

     To date two projects have been used as vehicles for
evaluating modern techniques- the new IRVR system for UK
airports and the ILS CSU.The Instrument Runway Visual Range

IRVR is a distributed system with field sensor units located at intervals along a runway to measure the prevailing visibility and report it back as a range value to ATC who in turn advise the aircraft pilots. The system must perform calibration routines, read sensors, make calculations using various laws and co-ordinate the reports from a number of locations.The IRVR is currently in operation at Heathrow and Gatwick airports.
The Categorisation and Status Unit is to be used to collect status information from the ILS equipment at each end of the runway, information about the runway in use, calculate the prevailing category of the ILS facility, and advise ATC. The CSU is expected to be completed in February 1989.

The IRVR Development
The IRVR specification called for the software to be documented and tested to meet the Level 2 requirements of DO-178A[3].The specification also recommended the use of ISO Pascal to support a planned application of the SPADE toolset as a means of gaining a level of assurance for the software. The minimum use of global variables was specified and hardware and software interrupts or concurrent processing was to be avoided.Of those companies invited to tender only one felt able to accept all of these constraints.
    Following agreement on the requirement specification an attempt was made to produce a top level design skeleton written in Pascal which could be verified using SPADE before any code was written. This process was not completed for lack of resources. Efforts to achieve design visibility through the production of data flow and structure diagrams were also frustrated by a lack of tools held by the developer to produce and maintain such diagrams. Another concession was to permit the use of the C language for the lower level routines even though we were advised that C was not suitable for high integrity software[1,2]
    The process improved as the developers became more familiar with the use of the SPADE tools.The software was written in SPADE-Pascal to allow flow analysis during development and its subsequent semantic analysis by an independent external reviewer. This meant that each procedure was annotated with formal comments giving the dependency relationships and global annotations. The global annotations specify those variables used in the procedure but not declared within the procedure's body or parameter list. The dependency relationship describes the imported and exported variables of the procedure. Errors were found by flow analysis during development and corrected.
    At mid project, the developer was requested to supply a significant segment of the code and its associated documentation for validation by an independent reviewer. The analysis high lighted shortcomings in the way the plain English software design description was being transformed into coded modules. It also revealed the incorrect implementation of a number sort routine. Improvements were made by the developer, and an improvised configuration management arrangement was set up. Finally the system was integrated and subjected to factory acceptance testing which

it passed without any problems. The software and its
documentation was then passed to the validator for
validation. This was a semi- formal method which relied on
program walk-throughs supported by semantic analysis.

Results   of Validation

The task of validation was tackled in two main stages.The
field equipment was validated first, followed by the centre
equipment. At the time of writing both tasks have been
completed except for some outstanding queries to be answered
by the designer. A final round-up report will be completed
following a full review of the project. The main points to
emerge are as follows.

Through the use of SPADE-Pascal, the validator has been
able to perform a validation of the software used in the IRVR
system. He has been able to trace the requirements from the
top-level documentation through to the SPADE - Pascal
implementation.This resulted in an exchange of questions and
answers between the validator and the design engineer,
ultimately providing NATS with a satisfactory level of
assurance for this system. This is already a major step
forward.

There were however a number of reservations in this,
mainly resulting from the manner of presentation of the
software and the lack of a "top level" software design
description.For example,two documents had to be produced by
the validator which strictly should have been produced by the
developer; a Conformance Matrix and Global Variable Cross
reference.The designer was unable to avoid the use of global
variables as it is necessary to retain values from one cycle
of the program to the next. One consequence of this was that
the 'derives lists' for each procedure became tediously long
particularly in the higher level procedures.

Post design changes.

It was decided that any design changes arising after delivery
would be subjected to the same procedures and analysis as the
original system. This is still the case although the order of
events is more difficult to control once a system goes into
operational use. For example the system documentation will
not be altered formally until after the modifications have
been incorporated.

Size and cost.

The IRVR consists of 249 modules and 68k bytes of object
code. The estimated cost of meeting the verification and
validation requirements is about 25% of the capital cost of
which 10% was for independent V&V and 15% was for the project
overheads to support it . The project development time was 10
months. The independent V&V took an additional 40 man days.

The CSU development.

Experience from the IRVR project convinced us that the basic
approach was correct but that it needed to be more fully and
formally applied to realise the maximum benefits. The CSU
specification reflected this approach and spelled out the

prime requirement ie. that the developer had to build a
system which could be validated and which in turn had to be
shown to comply with the specification. The NATs
specification for the system was semi formal in nature as it
contained sets of tables describing the data relationships to
be used in calculating the ILS category. However, it was
decided to have a formal specification in VDM produced for
the system based on the NATS specification. The principal aim
of this task was to give us experience with VDM but it was
also consistent with an evolving belief that NATs
specifications should be subjected to third party review. A
secondary objective was that the developer should be able to
benefit from the VDM, and have their design verified with
respect to this. However, the plain English version of the
specification was used for contract purposes owing to the
developer's inexperience with VDM. Following open tender
action the contract for the CSU was awarded to the same
company which built the IRVR system.

By this time the impact of the IRVR project development
had been recognized within the company which now became
committed to formalising the techniques in their development
area. Provision was made within the contract for the company
to have design consultantcy particularly for the top level
design. Provision was also made for the top level design and
the software modules to be verified independently using
SPADE as they became available. During the project up to 30%
of the modules will be subject to additional static analysis
against the documentation as it exists at the time, and
finally a segment of the total system will be validated
against NATS specification.

Progress at the time of writing.

A VDM specification together with proof obligations was
produced for the system. A number of observations can be made
about this: The primary requirement - that of producing an
accurate and consistent statement of requirements and to
validate the procurement specification has been met. In the
process errors were found in the specification and in the VDM
specification although these were mainly of a syntactic
nature and discovered before the proof obligations were
constructed. This latter point highlights the need for tool
support to help with syntax checking of VDM.

The developer received the formal specification well
even though he did not have any specific training in VDM. The
alternative interpretation of the CSU logic in the document
provided the developer with added insight in producing a
system design specification. The operations written in VDM
are useful in the coding phase and are expected to save the
developer time in deriving similar operations to be coded
from the original English version of the specification. The
VDM specification also gives NATS the potential to verify
the code formally should we wish to do so.

Another point of interest was how well a VDM
specification might cope with change. Thus when a genuine
specification change did arise we delayed advising the VDM
writer until the formal specification was completed. In this

particular case the VDM specification was much easier to amend than the logic tables in the original specification.

The design phase.

Once the equipment performance specification was agreed and signed off formally to the developer the development proper began. Together with the consultant the basic concept for the design was agreed, and it was clear that it was to be a data processing system with no interrupts. The subsequent stages of the development are outlined in short form below:

In the top level design, data flow diagrams and structure diagrams are being prepared by hand and a computer aided design package is being used to produce and manage these. With advice from the consultants a top level design for the system functions is being prepared as an outline skeleton written in Pascal. The skeleton design is then subjected to SPADE flow analysis. Errors revealed by this process are corrected by the designer. The design documents also include a diagram depicting all the global variables and their uses. The procedures have been nested to assist with later analysis but also to minimise the length of the "derives" lists. A data dictionary has been produced listing the variables and the procedures which use them. At the time of writing, no code has been written. It is planned to carry out a mid project V&V and finally to carry out a V&V on selected modules.

CSU size and cost.

The current size estimate for the system software is 140 modules and 20k bytes of object code.Formal specification development, design consultantcy and through project verification is expected to cost between 10% and 15% of the capital cost . No provision has yet been made for a full validation of all the software by an independent reviewer.

SUMMARY OF THE RESULTS FROM PROJECTS TO DATE

For the size and nature of the projects considered we can produce analysable code and designs.The IRVR and the CSU will be much better documented than many of the systems we have procured before.

The IRVR has been trouble free during its first year of operation. We believe that the emphasis placed on the design phase brought significant benefits to the project. It is likely that some of the design techniques used will be applied to similar projects in the future regardless of whether they are safety related or not.

Although static analysis has been shown to be important there is still a strong case for dynamic testing. In the two projects considered above, the results of the path function analysis were not used in support of testing. It is planned to study this issue in the near future.

The IRVR and CSU whilst they are embedded systems are not totally representative of a Navaid system in either scale or complexity. However, the techniques are still applicable, and it would be a design aim with these more complex systems to partition the functions in such a way that it would enable the software representing these functions to be verified.

Cost has been shown to be a significant factor to be considered when deciding to pursue even a semi formal verification and validation. In considering this technology for a particular application, we may be forced to ask if we can afford it? Is it the only way to do it? Can we test and maintain it? These questions can only be answered when the circumstances of the application are known.

The approver will seek to assure that the system has been properly designed for its intended role and that the design includes features to minimise the risks. If software is included in these systems then the risk assigned to the software-based elements has to be identified and design solutions evolved accordingly. The reliance placed on the software will depend on the extent to which it can be verified and validated. In the end, approval will be granted for the total system and the software will be approved in that context.

REFERENCES

1. Carre B.A., "Safe" High order Languages.A discussion paper prepared by PVL for CAA - April 1987

2. Wichmann B.A,   Notes on the Security of Programming Languages.Paper prepared for CAA - May 1987

3. Radio Technical Commission for Aeronautics / DO-178A

4. NATO Allied Quality Assurance Publications /AQAP 1 & 13

5. DTI and NCC "The STARTS guide " Second edition 1987.

6. UK Ministry of Defence DEF STAN 0055. Draft expected for publication in 1989.

7. ACARD, Software - A vital key to UK competitiveness HMSO 1986.

ACKNOWLEDGEMENTS

The following companies were contracted by NATS in the projects referred to in this paper.

Program Validation Limited Southampton	Consultants to UK CAA member for ICAO. Contractors for IRVR V&V using SPADE.
John Bell Technical Systems Fleet.	Developer of VDM specification for CSU.

Aeronautical & General Instruments, Verwood, Dorset	Developer and manufacturer of IRVR and CSU
Royal Signals and Radar Establishment-RSRE, Great Malvern.	Analysis of systems software using MALPAS

6

CERTIFICATION OF SOFTWARE IN AIRBORNE SAFETY CRITICAL SYSTEMS - AN EQUIPMENT MANUFACTURER'S VIEWPOINT

I. N. SPALDING
Software Manager, Flight Control Systems
Smiths Industries Aerospace and Defence Systems
Bishops Cleeve, Cheltenham, Gloucestershire, GL52 4SF, UK

ABSTRACT

The growth in the application of digital computers for use in commercial aircraft and, in particular, the increase in the use of safety critical systems represents a major challenge to the aviation industry.

The techniques and methods that should be used in the development and management of software for airborne computer-based equipment are contained in RTCA document DO-178A. This document is used by the certification authorities as a basis for the certification of avionics software.

This paper looks at the certification process and, in particular, the requirements and interpretation of DO-178A for safety critical systems.

INTRODUCTION

The development of software for airborne systems is by necessity a demanding process especially for software embedded in safety critical systems. The guidelines for developing airborne software are contained in the document known universally as DO-178A [1]. Smiths Industries has had many years' experience in developing software for airborne systems, including several safety critical systems, and this paper is based on the experience gained in achieving certification of systems from a number of different regulatory authorities.

CERTIFICATION PROCESS

It may be interesting for those who are only involved in the software aspects of certification to look briefly at the certification process from an equipment manufacturer's viewpoint. The description below is only a general guide and the documents produced may vary by manufacturer, however, the process is essentially the same.

The overall certification requirements are normally defined in, or referred from, the customer specification. This specifies the environment in which the equipment is intended to function (e.g. temperature, vibration), and also refers to (or may state in detail) the airworthiness requirements for the country in which the aircraft is to be manufactured.

From the customer requirement the manufacturer will produce a design to meet the functional requirements and also will produce a plan detailing how it will be shown that the equipment achieves compliance with the requirements. This will include environmental requirements and those arising from airworthiness requirements. The environmental aspects will be documented in a Qualification Plan and the tests carried out by an approved test house (which may be independent or in-house) which produces a Type Test Report.

In addition, the manufacturer will produce a Certification Plan which will embody a Failure Modes and Effects Analysis (e.g. what is the effect of a component failure on the equipment and its rate of occurrence), a Failure Analysis (showing the rate of occurrence and the effects of equipment failure on the system), and a Safety Analysis (showing the rate of occurrence and the effects of a system failure on the aircraft in which it must be shown that the rate of occurrence must be less than that demanded by the criticality defined for the system). This latter document may be produced by the aircraft manufacturer. It may be appreciated that this process could be iterative in that if the system does not meet the criticality requirements then it would have to be modified or redesigned and the analysis repeated, and so on.

When the development has been completed, the equipment manufacturer would present the required documents either to the regulatory authority direct (if it is for equipment approval in its own right), or to the aircraft manufacturer for incorporation in their own documentation and then presentation to the authority. These documents may include the Functional Specification, Software and Hardware documents and drawings, Type Test Report and Configuration Index. For some aircraft manufacturers an additional document called the Declaration of Design and Performance (DDP) is also produced which is a summary from the manufacturer of what has been carried out during the development process.

SOFTWARE CERTIFICATION GUIDELINES

Relationship to Airworthiness Requirements

Before looking at the software certification guidelines in detail, it is worthwhile to see the relationship that exists between these and the Airworthiness Requirements.

The regulations covering aircraft, engines, propellers and so on are contained in documents called Joint Airworthiness Requirements (JARs) in Europe and Federal Aviation Requirements (FARs) in the United States. These two sets of standards are essentially the same although there are national differences. However, all paragraph numbering within the sets are the same in order to facilitate cross comparison. For the purposes of this paper only those regulations covering large aeroplanes will be considered and these are contained in JAR-25 (or FAR Part 25). JAR 25.1309 (or FAR

25.1309) covers Equipment, Systems and Installations [2] but does not contain any explicit reference to software. However, the Advisory Circular associated with this paragraph, ACJ No. 1 to JAR 25.1309 [3], contains interpretative material together with definitions of the terms associated with probabilities. It is here (and in the FAA Advisory Circular 25.1309-1) that the criticality categories and their associated probabilities are introduced and these are summarised in Table 1.

TABLE 1
Relationship between probability and severity of effects

Criticality Category		Required qualitative probability of malfunction	Required quantitative probability of malfunction (operating hours)
JAR-25	FAR Part 25		
Catastrophe	Critical	Extremely improbable	<1 in 10^9
Hazardous	Essential-major	Extremely remote	<1 in 10^7
Major	Essential-minor	Remote	<1 in 10^5
Minor	Non-essential	Reasonably probable	<1 in 10^3

In order to find the reference to the software certification guidelines it is now necessary to look at the Civil Aviation Authority (CAA) Airworthiness Notice No. 45A [4]. This states that the RTCA/EUROCAE Document DO-178A/ED12A ´Software Considerations in Airborne Systems and Equipment Certification´ is "acceptable as a basis for the certification of the software in aircraft systems and equipment". Similarly, the Federal Aviation Administration (FAA) Advisory Circular 20-115A [5] states that an applicant "may use the considerations outlined in RTCA Document RTCA/DO-178A as a means, but not the only means, to secure FAA approval of digital computer software".

Criticality Categories

The CAA Airworthiness Notice No. 45A also relates the software levels contained in DO-178A/ED-12A to the severity of the effect of software errors within the system or equipment (see Table 2). However, both this Notice and DO-178A state that "using appropriate design and/or implementation techniques and considerations it may be possible to use a software level lower than the functional categorisation." It is for this reason that DO-178A refers throughout specifically to software levels rather than criticality categories. It is interesting to note that DO-178A itself does not state probabilities - this is only done in ACJ No. 1 to JAR 25.1309. In fact DO-178A states that, at the time the document was written, there was no method which could estimate post-verification probability of software errors and for this reason no probabilities were included in the document.

TABLE 2
Relationship between function criticality category and software level

ACJ No.1 to JAR 25.1309 Definition of Criticality Category	Minor Effect	Major Effect	Hazardous Effect	Catastrophic Effect
FAA Advisory Circular 25.1309-1 Definition of Criticality Category	Non-essential	Essential		Critical
DO-178A/ED12A Software level	Level 3	Level 2		Level 1

History of DO-178A

Early in 1980 the Radio Technical Commission for Aeronautics (RTCA) established an ad hoc committee to look at the functional performance requirements for certification as covered in existing RTCA minimum performance standards and FAA technical standard orders. It found that additional guidance material was needed for software requirements and recommended that a special committee should be set up to develop and document software practices that would support the certification of software based systems and equipment. Special committee 145 ´Digital Avionics Software´ was formed in May 1980 and SC-145 produced RTCA document DO-178 ´Software Considerations in Airborne Systems and Equipment Certification´ which was approved and published in January 1982.

DO-178 was subsequently updated to reflect the experience gained in its use for certification and was re-issued in 1985 as RTCA document DO-178A. The corresponding European advisory body, the European Organisation for Civil Aviation Electronics (EUROCAE) approved it for European use in October 1985 with the same title and the reference RTCA DO-178A/EUROCAE ED-12A.

Summary of DO-178A

This paper will not describe in detail the contents of DO-178A but will summarize its main features as related to level 1 software.

As has previously been mentioned the document differentiates between the criticality categories of each function of the equipment or system and the level of software associated with these categories. Thus it classifies the criticality categories as critical, essential or non-essential and the software as level 1, level 2 or level 3. Normally level 1 is associated with a critical function, level 2 with essential, and so on. However, the document indicates that it may be possible to use a software level lower than the functional categorisation through the use of appropriate system design techniques. An example of such a technique is a critical function which has been implemented by two parallel sets of computing implemented dissimilarly in software where the overall system is critical but the software elements are level 2. Design errors are detected by comparison between the two lanes and in the event of a mismatch the system is switched off. Obviously such a simple example would not be appropriate for all critical applications. The document also makes the point that for certain critical systems, such as those used in fly-by-wire applications, other measures may be necessary, in addition to a high level of software discipline, in order to achieve the required system safety objectives.

The document uses a simple model to define the elements of the software development process that must be addressed for certification. The software life cycle is divided into:

- systems requirements
- software requirements
- software design
- implementation

and the verification activities are composed of analysis and test and consist of:

- software requirements versus system requirements
- software design versus software requirements
- code review versus software design and coding standards
- module testing and review
- software integration testing and review
- hardware/software integration testing and review

Finally the system undergoes system validation testing which provides confirmation of compliance of the implemented system with the total system requirements. Additionally, assurance of each of the development and verification processes must be given to the regulatory authorities in order to demonstrate compliance appropriate to the software level.

Level 1 software is naturally the most demanding and full assurance must be provided for each of the development and verification processes. An important part of demonstrating compliance at level 1 is to provide a traceability matrix linking all stages of development and verification which must then be audited in order to assess completion of all design and verification tasks. Additionally, a comprehensive problem tracking system must be used to ensure that all corrective actions are carried out.

For testing, the tests are divided into requirement based tests, which are derived from the software requirements independent of the software structure, and structure based tests which are used to complement the requirement based tests, in order to ensure that all parts of the software are exercised.

DO-178A outlines the development and certification of support software, in particular, where credit will be taken for its use. The document also describes the role of software configuration management, including change control, and software quality assurance as these disciplines are essential to ensuring the integrity of the product.

DO-178A finally lists the documents which are expected for software development and those which are required to support certification and gives a brief summary of each document's contents.

INTERPRETATION OF DO-178A

DO-178A has been shown to provide a good framework for the software development process for airborne software. However, there have been a number of areas which are not fully defined in the document and which, therefore, have been open to interpretation. Some of these are covered below.

Verification and Test Plans

Central to the certification process is the assurance and analysis that must be carried out for each development stage. DO-178A states that these should be contained in the document 'Software Verification Plan, Procedures and Results' and the policies, procedures and practices for carrying out the verification and testing will be contained in the document 'Software Quality Assurance Plan'. DO-178A only gives general guidance as to the contents of these documents and it has been found necessary to expand on the contents, in particular, for level 1 software.

The certification authorities require to see that the verification plan defines an overall strategy to the verification and testing activities covering the complete software development lifecycle and shows how the stages of verification or testing are complementary. For example, certain tests may be carried out at a module level because they cannot be performed at a higher level and this omission at the higher level must be justified. The rationale for carrying out each test, and if applicable the rationale for the choice of test input values must be detailed. For level 1 software the degree of structural coverage must be defined. Executing "each element of the software" (DO-178A terminology) may be insufficient and stronger criteria such as decision coverage, condition coverage or a combination of these should be considered. Finally an analysis must be carried out of the tests in order to ensure adherence to the detailed test plan and procedures and any deviation from the expected test results must be justified, or tests reworked, or additional tests performed. It should be noted that there should also exist an overall test strategy at the equipment level which addresses not only software but also the systems and hardware testing.

An important part of the plan and procedures is that they must show in advance of the verification testing what activities are planned to take place and how the verification activities cover all aspects of verification and testing required for the software criticality level.

The verification plan must also show the procedures and methods to be used during verification and testing and these must be in sufficient detail to ensure a commonality of approach across a project e.g. the use of standard check lists is encouraged. This also needs to cover the criteria for assessing if a test passes or fails and the analysis activities. Additionally, the environment for carrying out testing needs to be described (this point is described in more detail below).

It will be seen from the above that the amount of information that must be provided for level 1 software in terms of strategy, procedures, rationale and analysis is considerable and additionally it must be shown that the plans must be in place in advance of the verification and testing.

Traceability

A second major area where the regulatory authorities place great stress is that of traceability. For level 1 software traceability must be provided from the system requirements through all stages of development to the corresponding verification and test activities. Thus for each requirement, at whichever level of development that requirement originated, it must be possible to identify that the requirement has been tested. Furthermore, the verification traceability matrix must be analysed to ensure complete coverage and, if necessary, additional tests performed. Recent experience has also shown that the regulatory authorities wish to see for critical systems traceability extended to show how all requirements at the system level have been tested, that is, not only in software but also during systems testing or hardware testing. The regulatory authorities tend to use the traceability matrix as the main ´index´ into all levels of software development and verification and a good, readable and complete matrix can give a high level of confidence in the supplier´s development process. To this end, recent projects at Smiths Industries have held all traceability information on a computerised database, which allows various ways of sorting to aid visibility at each development level. Also on larger projects, cross reference information is embedded into the documentation and this traceability data is extracted automatically from the documentation and input into the database.

Support Software

One area where the guidance of DO-178A is not specific is that of support software. In recent years the contribution of support software towards certification has become increasingly important, particularly for level 1 software. DO-178A states that "the extent to which support software should be documented and verified depends on the degree of reliance made on the supporting software/hardware during certification". Support software covers compilers, assemblers, test harnesses and so on, some of which will have been bought "off-the-shelf" and others developed "in-house". The analysis of what contribution a support tool has towards certification can be difficult and the level of documentation and verification/testing that would then be required is not defined either in DO-178A or to the author´s knowledge, in other standards. Furthermore, for purchased software it is often difficult, if not impossible, to obtain such assurance even if was defined. The contribution of support tools is becoming of increasing importance and this is an area that requires better guidance. In the interim the equipment manufacturers must make their own proposals and obtain customer and certification authority approval.

Software Languages

No guidance is given to DO-178A as to the type of language to be used or whether a high order language is to be preferred over an assembly language. This is proper in that DO-178A is not the place to make such statements which are best left to the customer´s specification, or supplier´s preference. The regulatory authorities have certainly indicated a preference for high order languages unless timing considerations preclude their use. However, this must be weighed against DO-178A's requirement for level 1 software, which demands that structural testing must "have executed each element of the software". The term "element" is not defined, but is usually taken to mean that all machine instructions must be executed. This in turn means that an analysis of the assembly output from the high order language compiler may have to be performed in conjunction with suitable emulators or other specialised tools. This, to a certain extent, undermines one of the reasons for using a high order language.

A further consideration with some high order languages, such as Ada or some implementations of Pascal, is that the software written by the equipment manufacturer will be linked into software provided by the compiler manufacturer. Examples of this are schedulers, exception handlers, and library and initialisation routines, all of which must be verified to the same level as the equipment manufacturer's software. This is an area where few compiler manufacturers understand the certification requirements and are unwilling, or unable, to provide the required design and verification evidence specified in DO-178A and, therefore, guidance and pressure from the regulatory authorities would be welcomed.

Fault Trend Analysis

An area which DO-178A does not refer to, but which is being increasingly demanded by the regulatory authorities for level 1 software, is that usually called fault trend analysis, and in AQAP-13 [6] as deficiency trend analysis. The requirements for this have not been clearly stated, but are taken to mean plotting a graph of defects resolved against time and analysing, in some way, the development stage at which the defects occurred. In this way confidence is given that defects are cleared as early in the development cycle as possible and that the defects outstanding are zero (or sufficiently low) at certification. However, difficulties remain in this area, for example, it must be decided how to interpret changes in requirements requested by the customers as some tracking systems treat design changes differently from defects.

System Validation

DO-178A gives little guidance in this area and declares it beyond the scope of the document. However, as has been discussed above, system validation is an essential part of achieving certification. The contribution of system validation to the overall testing strategy must be presented and the traceability of system tests to the systems requirements must be shown. Again, recent experience has shown that the system validation must be treated in a similar manner to software verification and testing in terms of strategy, procedures, rationale and analysis, and include control and verification of the testing environment in just the same way as support software. There needs to be clearer guidance and greater stress should be placed on this area either in DO-178A or in a companion document covering systems aspects. Similarly, the contribution of hardware tests to the certification process must also be considered.

Other Systems Aspects

One point mentioned earlier in this paper is that DO-178A may be used as "a means, but not the only means" of securing certification. Furthermore, certain applications may require additional measures, other than those quoted in DO-178A, in order to achieve the required safety requirements. It would be helpful if further advisory material was available so that guidance could be given to the credit that would be obtained from using other techniques. An example of this would be for the types or degrees of dissimilarity in systems, hardware or software design.

General Procedures

DO-178A calls for a 'Software Quality Assurance Plan' to be produced which covers design policies, procedures and practices and also that the equipment manufacturer must have a separate Software Quality Assurance organisation. However, DO-178A makes no reference to the certification authorities requirement that the equipment manufacturer must demonstrate an adequate degree of planning, control and audit. These aspects are normally covered in a 'Software Development Plan' which in some organisations is the top document of the software documentation tree. This document would typically cover schedules, milestones, dependencies, manpower, methods and frequencies of reporting, monitoring and auditing and so on, all of which should give confidence that the software project is being planned and controlled adequately. Such a document is not required by DO-178A and the only required relevant data is a summary of milestones and development phases in the 'Accomplishment Summary'. Further thought needs to be given to the documentation structure and contents, particularly for large projects.

CONCLUSIONS

This paper has looked at the certification process and in particular how software certification is carried out for critical systems. It is felt that the framework that DO-178A provides is good for software development. However, experience gained over the years since its approval, trends in development methods, changes to and the appearance of other national and international standards, and the growth in the use of level 1 software, have meant that it is now time to consider updating DO-178A.

ACKNOWLEDGEMENTS

I would like to thank my colleagues at Smiths Industries for their help towards writing this paper. While the ideas expressed in the paper are personal, the processes described are based on standards and procedures used within Smiths Industries.

REFERENCES

1. 'Software Considerations in Airborne Systems and Equipment Certification'. US Radio Technical Commission for Aeronautics Document DO-178A/European Organisation for Civil Aviation Electronics Document ED-12A, 1985.

2. JAR 25.1309 and FAR 25.1309 'Equipment, systems and installations'.

3. ACJ No.1 to JAR 25.1309 'Definitions' and FAA Advisory Circular 25.1309-1 'Definition of Criticality Category'.

93

4. ´Software Management and Certification Guidelines´.   Civil Aviation Authority Airworthiness Notice No. 45A.

5. ´Radio Technical Commission for Aeronautics Document RTCA/DO-178A´. Federal Aviation Administration Advisory Circular No. 20-115A, 1986.

6. AQAP-13 NATO Software Quality Control System Requirements.

7

DEVELOPING SOFTWARE FOR CERTIFICATION

J.V.Hill

Rolls-Royce & Associates Ltd., PO Box 31, Derby DE2 8BJ, U.K.

INTRODUCTION

Rolls-Royce and Associates have designed plant which involves microprocessor based systems, including software, which control plant operations critical to safety. Before such software can be used, it is necessary to satisfy a third party that the plant will operate safely. It is thus, in effect, necessary to certify the software.

THE ROLE OF CERTIFICATION

What must be borne in mind, however, is that the objective of any software development is not that it can be certified - it is that the software should be "fit for purpose". If this has been done, the certification should follow as a consequence. There is a difficulty, however, in defining what is "fit for purpose". As yet there are no internationally or nationally agreed standards against which the software can be assessed. Various steps are being made in this direction with the proposed DEF STAN 00-55, IEC 880 from the EEC, and the recommendations of the recent ACARD report from the DTI. However, there is as yet no sign that these various initiatives will lead to a single standard by which customers for software, developers of software and certification authorities can judge the product.

Examining the issue from a different perspective, there is still within UK industry as a whole a lack of awareness of the potential problems which could be caused by inadequately developed software, and of the various techniques which can be used to improve the software development process. Those industries which are at the forefront of this issue, in which software may be used in safety critical or security related applications, already require some type of "approval" of the total product. This may be given by the customer themselves, such as the government, or by a third party appointed by the customer, such as the CAA. Thus it could be argued that certification acts as a catalyst in formulating attitudes towards software development, and as such is likely to be of benefit to the software industry as a whole. The phenomenon of software projects being 90% complete for 50% of the time indicates that, such a catalyst is certainly required.

AGREEING CERTIFICATION STANDARDS

The above comments lead to the conclusions that for some
applications certification is already required, yet there are
no existing sets of standards against which this
certification can be achieved. So how do we proceed from
this position? At the present time it is necessary to spend
significant time over a long period in discussion with
appropriate regulatory bodies in order to define appropriate
methods. These cover both developing software in such a way
as to ensure its correct operation, and further demonstrating
that this has been achieved. These discussions must take
place before development commences to agree methods which
will be used, during development, to ensure that all parties
fully understand those methods, and following development to
provide the final assurance that the software is "fit for
purpose".

CHANGING STANDARDS

This process, of course, takes place during a phase of
continually developing and changing ideas within the software
industry in general about the way in which safety critical
software should be developed. Issues such as diversity,
formal methods and proof of correctness, and reliability
measurement of software are all areas of current debate. In
this situation it is always necessary to define what methods
are to be used at the start of a project, and then to stick
to them, if a project is to be successfully completed. It
can mean however, that a subsequent project may well use a
different set of methods, and what was "right" for
certification two years ago will not be seen as such today.
This is a measure of the lack of maturity of the industry
compared to the longer standing disciplines of, say,
electrical engineering, with consequent rapid improvements in
development methods.

DEFINING CATEGORIES OF SOFTWARE

The following discussion addresses the methods RRA have used
to develop software for safety critical applications. The
first stage of this process is to decide what is a safety
critical application. It is evident that the product as a
whole must operate safely. However, various parts of the
system may have more or less significance in effecting this
safe operation.

Software can be used at many different levels of
functionality. It can be used to collect data for subsequent
analysis, to give warnings or alarms to operators to indicate
some action is required, or to directly take action itself to
ensure the plant is safe. The degree to which it is
necessary to be confident that the software will operate
correctly varies depending on its use.

Thus the first step of the development of safety critical
software is a hazards analysis, to determine the level of
requirement. The process would be simpler, and much less
open to debate, if the hazards analysis could provide a
totally quantitative guideline, which could then be matched
to a set of software development techniques which guarantee a
numerical value of reliability which could be measured
against the guideline. In practice, however, RRA have not
found this to be the case. Probabilistic Risk Assessment can
be used to provide a guideline as to the requirements for
safe operation of component systems. Hardware component
failures can be analysed to provide FMEA's (Failure Modes and
Effects Analysis). These techniques address the problems of
the consequences of failure of a system, and the occurrence
of a fault in a particular system component. They do not,
however, address the issue of design errors, which is seen as
being a significant problem in software. There are two
options for examining this - quantify the effect of the
design error, or reduce the number of errors below the
threshold of detectability. RRA has adopted the second
option, and thus has taken the approach that the criteria
against which the software development process is judged are
qualitative and not quantitative.

SOFTWARE DEVELOPMENT METHODS

For safety critical and high reliability software RRA have
defined methods which consist of a "kit of parts", the
appropriate elements of which are used depending on the
application type, and the applicability of the element.
These elements relate to the standard software lifecycle
development process.

Particular emphasis has been placed on the specification and
validation areas of software development. Specification
methods use the techniques of formal specification and
animation (prototyping), in order to obtain the maximum
confidence in the definition of the software. The formal
specifications are then combined with static analysis to
prove the software against the original definition. Programs
are written in a limited sub-set high level language to
increase confidence in this operation, and structured design
and analysis techniques are used. Programs are validated
using statistically based dynamic testing techniques.

It is important to note that these techniques are not
alternatives, but each adds some element of assurance of the
correct operation of the software. Thus for the safety
critical applications formal language specification and
proving through static analysis and validation using
statistically based derived data and diverse implementation
used during the validation process are employed. It is
worthy of note that in the more recently completed projects
which used these techniques no errors were found during the
proving and validation stages - they had effectively been
removed during specification, development and testing. It

could thus be argued that one or other of these stages was unnecessary. However, the latter stages are used to <u>demonstrate</u> that the quality achieved from the former is adequate. The former stages are designed to maximise the confidence that no errors are found in the latter. Thus the techniques are complementary.

As noted previously, in developing software the objective is to seek an optimum engineering solution to a problem, rather than that which with the minimum effort and cost satisfies the certification requirements. However, the need for demonstration of the adequacy of the design inevitably means that there is some "design for certification" - the software must be designed to allow for simple demonstration.

RRA EXPERIENCE

As stated earlier we have recently completed a project using the techniques outlined above. The system underwent full integration testing with the identification of a small number of hardware design errors, but no software design errors. The software successfully passed through all its validation tests with no problems discovered. It was also developed to estimated timescale and cost. It is thus of interest to examine which factors in the development process were significant in achieving this. Six can be identified:-

a) Feedback between the animation of the formal specification and the engineer who defined the original requirement significantly reduced the number of errors in the specification, before software development was even commenced.

b) The development of test cases for the animation ensured that the operational range of the application had been considered before software development was commenced, and provided the basis of the test cases to be used during development.

c) The use of static analysis tools within the development, in addition to their use as a validation tool, assisted in the development of structured software, and ensured that the product could be easily validated.

d) The use of full automatic configuration control <u>during</u> development, rather than just on completion of certain stages of development, reduced the number of induced errors, particularly in a situation in which a large project team was involved over a short period of time.

e) The full commitment of all staff to the methods used and their potential benefits, is significant. Methods can always be circumvented by staff unwilling or unprepared to use them.

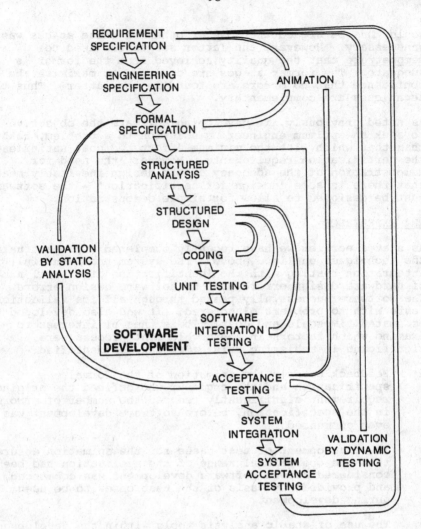

REQUIREMENT
SPECIFICATION

ENGINEERING
SPECIFICATION

ANIMATION

FORMAL
SPECIFICATION

STRUCTURED
ANALYSIS

STRUCTURED
DESIGN

VALIDATION
BY STATIC
ANALYSIS

CODING

UNIT TESTING

SOFTWARE
INTEGRATION
TESTING

SOFTWARE
DEVELOPMENT

ACCEPTANCE
TESTING

SYSTEM
INTEGRATION

VALIDATION
BY DYNAMIC
TESTING

SYSTEM
ACCEPTANCE
TESTING

f)   The specification included requirements for the fault
     tolerance and defensive programming techniques to be
     used, rather than leaving these at the discretion of the
     development team.

The Figure 1 demonstrates the total specification,
development and validation cycle.

SUMMARY

Summarising the above discussion, several points can be
made:-

1.   The techniques used by RRA to develop software
     successfully achieved a product to time, to cost and
     which passed all its validation tests to demonstrate
     both its structural and operational quality.

2.   These techniques were used because of the safety
     critical nature of the software.

3.   The software has to be accepted by a certifying
     authority, but there are as yet no nationally or
     internationally agreed standards to guide either the
     authority, the developer, or the customer.

4.   The total costs over the specification, development and
     system integration cycle were no more than for
     comparable projects where these techniques were not
     used. The distribution of costs, however, was
     significantly redistributed towards the initial stages.
     The project successfully demonstrated that where the
     effort was put in initially, and full configuration
     control was used during development, the 90% complete
     for 50% of the time syndrome was avoided.

CONCLUSIONS

The final point could be of significance to the software
industry as a whole. Could the techniques currently being
developed for safety critical software development actually
be of use for improving the achievement of industry in
developing projects to timescales and costs? For this to be
true, all those involved require commitment to the methods,
which is certainly not currently the case. An increased role
for software certification for many types of application may
well be the necessary catalyst to lead to the change of
software development from an immature industry to a fully
established engineering discipline.

8

SOFTWARE SAFETY CERTIFICATION IN POTENTIALLY HAZARDOUS INDUSTRIES

CHRIS DALE
National Centre of Systems Reliability,
United Kingdom Atomic Energy Authority,
Wigshaw Lane, Culcheth, Warrington WA3 4NE, UK

ABSTRACT

This paper discusses particular problems of software safety certification in potentially hazardous industries, based on relevant experience of similar problems in the nuclear industry. As in other branches of engineering, the advent of computers and advanced technology more generally has resulted in opportunities for safe and reliable systems control which go beyond that which could previously be achieved. The nuclear industry world-wide has adopted these new technologies cautiously, in part because of the intrinsic difficulties involved in justifying the safety of software-based systems. The UKAEA is involved in a range of research and development activities concerned with issues related to software certification. This includes topics such as software reliability assessment, formal specification of real-time systems, and experimental work on the testing of ultra-high reliability systems. This work, and its relevance to future software certification activities in potentially hazardous industries, will be described.

INTRODUCTION

The purpose of this paper is to discuss the safety certification of systems containing software which are used in potentially hazardous industries, and to describe relevant work being carried out by the United Kingdom Atomic Energy Authority. The systems under consideration include any in which software resident within the system has potential impact upon the safe operation of the system: the assessment of software used for the design of systems, such as the computer programs used for the shield design of UK power reactors, is also important, but is not within the scope of the paper.

After discussion of some general certification issues, there is a review of software certification activities in the nuclear industry, and a summary of relevant UKAEA research. The paper concludes by discussing the relevance of the nuclear experience to certification of software in other potentially hazardous industries.

GENERAL ISSUES

What is Software Certification?
A number of types of engineering system are subject to certification requirements, often motivated by safety concerns: examples include civil aircraft requiring a certificate of airworthiness, and nuclear power plant which require a licence to operate. Where certification covers aspects of these systems which include software, such as may be the case with avionics, the question of software certification arises in a natural way – irrespective of the fact that the need to certify certain kinds of engineering system has existed for many more years than has the use of computer software in these systems. Despite this, there is in general no clear agreement on even the meaning of software certification, not to mention the question of how it should be carried out.

Certification of compilers for programming languages such as Pascal is carried out by submitting the compiler in question to a fixed series of tests, and confidence in the integrity of the compiler in general is dependent upon the assumption that these tests represent a large proportion of the functionality of the compiler. There is clearly an (unstated) limit to the reliance which can be put on a product certified in this way; for safety-critical applications, compilers should also be mature, in the sense that their performance and properties are well-understood on the basis of extensive usage.

Certification of software correctness is another appealing notion which does not stand up to close examination. There is no such thing as a correct piece of software, in an absolute sense; software can be correct only with respect to something, such as a specification. Given that the specification in question is a formal one, it is in principle possible to prove that the software is correct with respect to its specification; in practice, this can be done only in a very restricted sense. A further problem here is that the specification is itself an abstraction of a volatile 'real world' requirement, and that abstraction may be imperfect.

For the purposes of this paper, software certification will be defined as the assessment of equivalence between the actual service delivered by the software, and its specified service. In certifying the safety of software, concern is with those aspects of service which have a potential impact upon safety.

What is the Problem?
The widespread use of computers in engineering systems of all kinds has been prompted by the practical capability of computers in dealing with complex logical requirements in an economic, reliable way. Modification of software (in a properly controlled manner, with suitable validation and verification checks) is easier than for a corresponding hard-wired system; and more information can be provided to operators than would be conceivable without using computer technology. These are the reasons that have persuaded engineers to adopt computer technology in preference to hard-wired digital and analogue hardware, despite the reputation for undependability which software systems have earned [1].

In many senses, software is very different from hardware, and it is these differences which determine the need to give special attention to the certification of software. Parnas et al [1] discuss these differences in detail: they identify problems of complexity, error sensitivity, difficulty of testing, correlation of failures, and lack of professional standards.

Complexity: This is the most obvious difference between software and hardware – it is often because a task is too complex to be practicable in hardware that a software solution is chosen.

Error sensitivity: This is that property of software which leads to large changes in system behaviour as the result of apparently trivial changes in circumstances – the engineering concept of 'tolerance' has no meaning for software.

Testing difficulty: Software is unarguably difficult to test adequately – one reason for this is that interpolation of test results to situations lying 'between' two tests is simply untrustworthy.

Correlation of failures: Seemingly independent pieces of software programmed against the same specification have a surprising proportion of common errors [2]. This imposes severe limitations on what can be expected from diversity in software based systems, though it is clear that some level of reliability improvement can be confidently anticipated [3].

Lack of professional standards: There are no accredited software engineers, in the way that there are in other engineering disciplines – simply because the discipline has still to mature sufficiently.

It can be seen from the above that there are many intrinsic difficulties with the process of software certification, caused by the very nature of software.

Software Safety Certification

The discussion so far has made little mention of safety or reliability; henceforth, the focus will be on the certification of safety of systems which are dependent upon software for their operation.

Safety and reliability are closely linked concepts, but it is important to distinguish between the certification that a given level of reliability has been achieved, and certification that a particular system is safe. A software reliability analysis is typically concerned with attempting to quantify the frequency with which failures are likely to occur; software safety analysis is concerned rather with the identification of links between the software and system safety hazards.

The definition of software certification given earlier leads to certification on the basis of direct observation and measurement of functional and non-functional attributes of the software. Thus it is not valid to certify a product solely on the basis of its development process: a product can be certified only if the product is examined, and any information about the development process should be used in support of the product examination. Indeed, in safety-critical applications, it is probable that certification on the basis of product attributes alone can never be achieved – the knowledge that the process is acceptable should be a pre-requisite to certification of the product.

Similarly, there is an important distinction between the achievability of a particular level of reliability, and the demonstration that this level has been achieved in practice: there is a difference between building a safe system, and demonstrating that a safe system has been built. There is no doubt that the proper application of software engineering techniques can sometimes produce very reliable software, which will not lead to a safety hazard when embedded within a particular system. The fact that the best techniques have been used does not however, of itself, enable any statement to be made concerning the level of reliability associated with a particular product - though, potentially at least, it may be possible to talk about the level of reliability which may be expected from typical products of a certain kind, given that a particular development strategy had been adopted. Demonstration of the reliability of a given product can only be attained by measurement of the reliability of that particular product.

Thus certification that a given level of reliability has been achieved by a particular product is possible only on the basis of either actual product operation (possibly as part of some overall system) or by a regime of testing which can be related to actual use. The only known way of relating software testing environments to usage is to mimic usage (or various kinds of usage) in the testing environment. This is in itself a very challenging activity, which limits the extent to which software reliability measurement is of value to certification.

It must be emphasised that certification of the proper application of a given development process does not constitute a certification of software reliability or safety. Though it is reasonable to expect that a high quality development will usually lead to a high quality product, this cannot be guaranteed.

Is Software Safety Certification Necessary?

There are three main barriers to certification of software safety in the context of a particular system: technical difficulties, the cost involved, and lack of visibility of the software. The first is dealt with elsewhere, and the second is significant, but outside the scope of the paper. The third typically arises where a piece of computer-controlled equipment is purchased for use in a safety critical area of an industrial plant, and the supplier is unwilling or unable to provide the necessary technical details to enable certification of the software aspect.

This is no small difficulty, especially when one bears in mind that safety critical Programmable Electronic Systems are often identical to those used outside the safety critical area; manufacturers will clearly lose interest in a comparatively small market with special demands in terms of certification. There is no easy answer to this problem in the general case.

There is a solution to the problem available in many particular instances. It is often the case that careful design at the system level can reduce or eliminate dependence of safety on the software. For example, mechanical or electrical interlocks can sometimes be employed to prevent the system from carrying out dangerous instructions erroneously generated by the software.

This serves to illustrate the need to consider certification needs of the system as a whole, and demonstrates that the barriers to certification can be overcome in economic ways, provided systems are well designed.

THE USE OF COMPUTERS IN THE NUCLEAR INDUSTRY

Within the nuclear industry, computers have been used for many years in normal plant control and monitoring systems, and are being introduced into safety related information systems. In France and Germany nuclear power stations have been licensed which use computers in their protection systems. The extent to which these various kinds of systems need to be certified clearly depends upon their impact on safety, and several classification schemes have been suggested, each with graded requirements [4]. There has been a tendency for the necessary certification methods to be developed separately within each country, due in part to local differences in licensing laws, with bodies such as the International Atomic Energy Agency (IAEA) providing mechanisms for discussion and harmonisation where appropriate.

Licensing in the UK

There are no UK power reactors which use protection systems which are wholly computer based; Sizewell B will be the first to have a primary protection system which is computer-based, while retaining a more 'traditional' secondary protection system. There are reactors which use computers in other safety related roles (such as refuelling in the newer Advanced Gas Cooled Reactors), and there is a good deal of research into the particular difficulties associated with the use of computers in safety related roles within nuclear power stations.

Licenses to operate nuclear power stations are granted by the Health and Safety Executive (HSE), advised by the Nuclear Installations Inspectorate (NII). It is the responsibility of the prospective licensee (normally the Central Electricity Generating Board (CEGB)) to demonstrate an acceptable level of safety.

The CEGB uses its Design Safety Criteria [5] and Design Safety Guidelines [6] in applying for a license: these expect the use of probabilistic risk assessment to quantify the performance of reactor protection systems, and at present propose the use of what is known as the 'common mode cut off'. This is a lower limit of 10^{-5} per demand on the probability of system failure due to causes such as fire, explosion, maintenance and design faults; in practise the value 10^{-5} is accepted only under extreme circumstances and where it has been justified - the more usual number is 10^{-4}, and where software is concerned 10^{-3} may be a more prudent figure at the current time. The aim of such a limit is to cater for the possible limitations of redundancy in achieving high reliability. It also acknowledges the potential for design errors, which may well lie in the software if the system is computer based. A consequence of the common mode cut off is that a secondary form of protection must be provided for the most frequent faults, in contrast with current practice in both France and the USA.

Another important principle used in the UK particularly is that of fail-safety: this is a design principle which demands that failures have a safe effect. This often means that failures are detected as they occur, with the plant then being moved to a safe condition.

To adjudge an application for a license, the NII use their safety assessment principles [7], which include the following points.

1. No single failure of the protection system should prevent its operation.

2. Appropriate and safe limits should be identified for protection parameters, and satisfactory operation shown within these limits.

3. Direct measurements are preferred to indirect ones.

4. Unforeseen events do occur, so adequate redundancy and diversity should be provided.

5. When the reliability requirements are very high and there are doubts about the systems reliability, then diversity should be provided.

6. Only proven components should be used.

7. Unsafe failures of the system should be alarmed when reasonably practicable.

Licensing overseas

Ehrenberger and Bloomfield have prepared a detailed review of licensing issues associated with the use of computers in the nuclear industry [4]. The review looks in detail at the USA, the UK, Germany and France; some of the important findings are outlined below.

In the USA there is a relatively large amount of experience concerning the licensing of computer based nuclear reactor protection systems: three such systems have been licensed - the first of these only after a complete re-write following rejection. Licensing is carried out by the Nuclear Regulatory Commission (NRC), who audit an argument of high quality produced by the licensee; there is an implicit assumption that computer technology can be adequately engineered for nuclear reactor protection systems. The detailed approach used by the NRC has developed over the last decade, as each of the three systems in question has passed through the licensing process. The NRC Licensing activity in respect of the Westinghouse Integrated Protection Systems will be discussed in greater detail later in the paper.

France is arguably the most advanced country in the world as far as the use of computers in reactor safety systems is concerned. The main systems which have been licensed are listed below.

1. <u>SPIN</u>: A pressurised water reactor protection system.

2. <u>CONTROBLOC</u>: A plant control and supervision system, also for use in pressurised water reactors.

3. <u>TCI</u>: An operator support system.

4. <u>TRTC</u>: A fuel element monitoring system used on the Superphenix fast reactor.

5. The self-test part of the Superphenix protection system - the essential aspects of the protection system itself are hard-wired.

The development of computer based protection systems in France is carried out according to standards developed in parallel with the SPIN system [8], which has a great deal in common with the related international standard [9]. Criteria for the licensing of these systems include the demand that programs must have simple structures, the avoidance of high level languages and operating systems, prototyping of systems, and review activities at software and systems level. Also important are the use of good quality equipment, exhaustive functional testing, good team organisation, and independent verification.

The French are particularly keen on the testability of the systems they build: this enables post-maintenance testing to be carried out in an economic way, to show that unchanged software continues to function properly after the addition, removal or modification of other parts of the system.

In countries other than those mentioned above, the use of computers in safety-related aspects of nuclear power is less well developed, but the same trend towards their use is present world-wide - further detail can be found in [4]. It can be seen that there are very different approaches to the licensing of such systems: the British demand a functionally diverse protection system to guard against failures caused by the computer based one, whereas the French and Americans are happy that the requisite levels of reliability can be achieved with computers alone; of the three, only the French demand the avoidance of high level languages.

The Westinghouse Integrated Protection System

The Westinghouse IPS is a complete integrated control and protection system for pressurised water reactors (PWR) [10]. It is of particular interest as it has been the subject of licensing activities in both the USA and UK. The American experience will be summarised first, then that in the UK.

The IPS makes extensive use of microprocessors for both safety functions and other aspects of control. Self-test facilities are also built into the system, providing some reassurance against the possibility of maintenance-induced failures. The software consists of 60,000 lines of high-level source code, and was developed with the use of independent verification and validation.

The US NRC evaluated the system by carrying out eight audits through the development cycle, from system design specification to system test. The detailed review was restricted to certain functions and parameters, which they traced through the development process. The objective was to evaluate the Westinghouse V&V process, examining faults found for evidence of problem areas. In addition to the audits, a sneak analysis [11] was carried out to analyse part of the communications software which had been written in assembler.

The above audits did not address the question of design diversity, and in order to do this, the NRC developed and applied a set of defence in depth and diversity guidelines [11]. These guidelines provide rules for determining which combinations of failures of functional units or blocks should be studied, taking account of interdependence between blocks; and address requirements for independence between plant systems, and their tolerance to common failures of two of more functional units.

The NRC gave Provisional Design Approval for the IPS, concluding that the strategy of independent V&V and review was very effective, leading to a highly reliable system.

The Sizewell B PWR will have a Primary Protection System (PPS) provided by Westinghouse, which is in fact a development of the IPS. The differences between IPS and PPS include updating of the hardware, use of a different high level language for the software, improved redundancy, and a greater emphasis on fail safety. Although neither formal methods nor a specification language has been used directly changes in the software development methodology do include greater emphasis on specification, on verification in the early stages, and on tools generally.

The NII consider the overall protection system to be acceptable, and accepts in principle the use of microprocessor technology for reactor protection [12]. They have not yet made a judgement as to the acceptability of the PPS, but have identified several areas of concern, including the need for a thorough check of the reiterated software [13]. The CEGB have also accepted the principle of microprocessor based reactor protection, seeing advantages in terms of the trip algorithms which will be possible, the provision of information to operators, and testing facilities; they also recognise the need for a careful independent assessment [14].

RELEVANT UKAEA RESEARCH

The ISAT Fail-safe Protection System

The principle of fail-safety is at the centre of nuclear reactor safety assessment in the UK, and ISAT (Individual Sub-Assembly Temperature monitoring) is a highly reliable fail-safe monitoring system developed by UKAEA for fast reactor applications [15]. This system multiplexes and interleaves test and actual input signals in such a way that a dynamic output signal containing a unique pattern is generated. This pattern is examined by hard-wired pattern recognition logic, and any discrepancy causes a trip signal to be generated: the occurrence of a correct pattern in the presence of hardware failures is inconceivable. This design leads to a system which can be shown to be fail-safe without recourse to a detailed Failure Modes and Effect Analysis - normally indispensible in the fail-safety area.

The ISAT system is also claimed to guard against failures caused by faults in software, but the validity of this claim is subject to some reservations: there must be no missing paths in the software, for example. Thus the claim can only be substantiated for very simple software based systems, of which ISAT is one.

Current UKAEA research at Winfrith is examining ways in which the ISAT principle can be extended to more complex algorithms, such as those utilised in the protection of PWR reactors. One idea which is being studied involves the use of inverse algorithms: outputs of the core protection algorithm are fed as inputs to a process whose aim is to calculate what the input values should have been. These 'calculated' inputs are then themselves fed through the protection algorithm. If all is well, such a system is stable (since it alternately processes real and recalculated input values): any divergence from this stability can be used as an error detection mechanism.

There is still much development work to be done on these ideas: problems to be solved include derivation of inverses for some complicated functions, and the multiplicity of inverses which exist for some relatively simple functions. Despite these problems, the approach is one which forces diversity into the design of the system, in such a way that the two diverse implementations are not even processing the same data.

SPECK
SPECK is a formal specification tool developed by the UKAEA at Harwell, in response to the need for an unambiguous, complete and self-consistent description of the requirements of a typical fast reactor safety system. The particular technical difficulties include several thousand input signals, time critical responses, and relatively complex algorithms.

A mathematical system model is built in a hierarchical fashion, to such a level that each subsystem performs a single transformation on a single input to produce a single output. A particular strength of SPECK is that it permits the modelling of temporal aspects of the specification, and so enables deadlocks and response times to be analysed.

The user interface to SPECK attempts to bridge the gap between tractability to plant engineers, and the need for mathematical formality. Possible future work includes the incorporation of safety and reliability requirements within the formal framework.

Guidelines on Reliability and Safety Assessment of Software (GRASS)
As part of the Alvey Software Reliability Modelling project, the National Centre of Systems Reliability (NCSR) within UKAEA is collaborating in the development of a set of guidelines to aid in the assessment of safety and reliability of systems. GRASS will provide a framework for the assessment of the software aspect, within the context of an overall systems assessment.

In assessing the safety of a particular system, it is essential to consider first the quality of the process which led to the development of that system - ideally, this should be done in parallel with the development, to avoid loss of information. This aspect of the assessment is not adequate in itself to justify certification of an individual product, but it is necessary to establish that the care taken in system development is commensurate with the safety requirements placed upon the system. In addressing this aspect of assessment, GRASS will detail what the assessor should be looking for as positive or negative indicators during the development process.

A second aspect which can be assessed is the product itself - in the case of software, various static analyses can be carried out on the source code which provide further evidence to support that gathered during the process assessment. Here, GRASS will advise on the interpretation of outputs from static analysis tools of various kinds, and give basic guidance on techniques such as software fault tree analysis [16].

The final aspect is assessment of the product behaviour, typically by testing it in an environment as similar as possible to that in which it will ultimately be used. GRASS will give guidance on the methods which can be used here, covering software reliability growth models [17-19] and less sophisticated but often more desirable methods based on simple sampling theory and Poisson statistics [1, 20].

It is anticipated that GRASS will have an important role to play in the certification of software based systems, in a range of potentially hazardous industries.

REQUEST (Reliability and Quality of European Software Technology)
Both NCSR and Winfrith participate in REQUEST, which is an ESPRIT project which aims to provide improved and validated techniques for measuring and modelling software quality and reliability, supported by appropriate prototype tools. The primary concern is with developing metrics and models which span as much of the development life-cycle as possible from specification to life-use, and with providing useful and timely information for project and quality management decision making and control.

The work of REQUEST is of significance to certification in varying degrees: of particular importance to the certification of safety is the work which has been carried out on the reliability modelling of high-reliability systems, where there have been important advances in the modelling of dependence between different versions of software carrying out the same functions [21-23].

SCOPE (Software Certification Scheme in Europe)
Both NCSR and Winfrith will be collaborating in the ESPRIT-2 project SCOPE, which aims to provide a technically validated and legally recognised European software certification procedure. The project will be concerned with the establishment of certification technology relying on product certification: the direct assessment of the adequacy of the actual service provided by the software versus its specified service. SCOPE will lead to the provision of certification services for software-based systems, in a variety of industries.

APPLICATION TO OTHER HAZARDOUS INDUSTRIES

The nuclear industry worldwide has obtained a great deal of experience in dealing with the problems of using software in safety-related and safety-critical systems. It is both likely and desirable that other hazardous industries will draw on this experience in dealing with these problems: this will be a continuation of a long established trend for reliability and safety issues to be addressed very early by the nuclear industry, with the lessons learnt being applied in industry more generally.

In the case of software certification, it has been seen above that there is wide acceptance of the ability of computer-based systems to achieve the levels of reliability required within safety-critical applications; the only reservation in this area is that some countries (including the UK) demand an additional 'back-up' system in the most critical areas. There are however wide differences between the principles adopted in various countries in an attempt to minimise the risk of failing to achieve the necessary levels of reliability.

To demonstrate these differences, consider the question of choice of implementation language. In France, high-level languages and compilers must be avoided; in the UK high-level languages are generally preferred, with the caveat that widely-used and thus well-validated compilers must be utilised; in the USA Westinghouse employed a specially created high-level language for their IPS, thereby accepting the lack of a widely-used compiler.

This example serves to illustrate a common software engineering theme - wide, even contradictory, differences of opinion on the best solution to agreed problems. In this particular instance these policy differences limit the extent to which systems developed in one country will be found acceptable in others. If such policy differences grow up in potentially hazardous industries generally, there could be enormous barriers to international trade in such systems; one of the aims of the SCOPE project is that these policy differences should be avoided, at least in a European context.

A current example which may lead to such policy differences is provided by the UK defence industry, where they are moves to introduce formal mathematical methods of specification for all safety-critical software. This policy is based upon the implicit assumption that these formal methods of software development represent the best possible current practice, with respect to the development of safety-critical systems. This may be true, but it is certainly not an uncontroversial assertion.

Whatever the technical merits of particular software development methods, the important point is that certification of safety should rest upon the critical assessment of a safety justification. As pointed out above, policies which, in an insufficiently mature technology, demand that certain specific practices be either mandatory or forbidden, run into the danger that they will contradict each other. They will certainly lead to the adoption of incompatible standards in different geographical areas.

The licensing schemes for software based systems developed by various national bodies in the nuclear industry are all, broadly speaking, based on the review and appraisal of arguments of excellence - of both process and product. This framework allows both developer and licensor to adopt new methods as they become available, without the attendant danger of forcing the premature and normative adoption of particular standards and procedures. This is an important lesson which industry in general should adopt, particularly in view of the open market which will exist in Europe within a very few years.

The nuclear industry, almost from its very beginnings, has led the development of reliability and safety technologies, most of which are now employed to the benefit of a wide range of industries. The safety certification of systems containing software is a very immature discipline, but the nuclear industry had already developed a great deal of experience in tackling the particular problems, and continues to carry out a great deal of vital research in the area.

This background suggests that other potentially hazardous industries can now benefit by drawing on the experience of software safety certification built up within the nuclear industry.

ACKNOWLEDGEMENT

This work was supported in part by the Alvey Directorate, as part of the Software Reliability Modelling project (SE/072).

REFERENCES

1. Parnas, D.L., van Schouwen, A. and Kwan, P., Evaluation standard for safety criticality software. IAEA Meeting on Microprocessors in Systems Important to the Safety of Nuclear Power Plants, London, May 1988.

2. Knight, J.C. and Leveson, N.G., An experimental evaluation of the assumption of independence in multiversion programming. IEEE Trans Software Eng., 1986, SE-12, 96-109.

3. Bishop, P., Esp, D., Barnes, M., Humphreys, P., Dahll, G. and Lahti, J., PODS - an experiment in software reliability. IEEE Trans Software Eng., 1986, Se-12, 929-940.

4. Ehrenberger, W.D. and Bloomfield, R.E., Licensing issues associated with the use of computers in the nuclear industry. CEC Nuclear Science and Technology Final Report, GRS mbH, Cologne, March 1987.

5. Design safety criteria for CEGB nuclear power stations. Central Electricity Generating Board report HS/R167/81 (Revised), March 1982.

6. Pressurised water reactor design safety guidelines. Central Electricity Generating Board Report DSG2 (Issue A), April 1982.

7. Safety assessment principles for nuclear power reactors. HM Nuclear Installations Inspectorate, April 1979 (published by HMSO, July 1982).

8. Colart, J.M. and Grisollet, J., Safety requirements related to the software used in the safety systems of nuclear reactors. S.A.F. Report No. 32.

9. Software for computers in the safety systems of nuclear power stations. IEC, Geneva, 1985.

10. Gallagher, J.M., Software for computers in safety systems of nuclear power plants. Proc. SAFECOMP 1983, Pergamon Press.

11. A defense-in-depth and diversity assessment of the RESAR-414 integrated protection system. US Nuclear Regulatory Commission report NUREG-0493, 1979.

12. A review by HM Nuclear Installations Inspectorate of the Sizewell B preconstruction safety report. NII Report, HMSO, July 1982.

13. Sizewell B Public Enquiry: Proof of evidence on HM Nuclear Installations Inspectorate's view of the Central Electricity Generating Board's safety case. NII, HMSO, March 1983.

14. Sizewell B Public Enquiry: Proof of evidence by Central Electricity Generating Board, HMSO, 1983.

15. Keats, B.A., Failsafe criteria for computer-based reactor protection systems. Nuclear Energy, 1980, 19, 423-28.

16. Leveson, N.G. and Harvey, P.R., Analysing software safety. IEEE Trans. Software Eng., 1983, Se-9, 569-79.

17. Jelinski, Z. and Moranda, P.B., Software reliability research. In Statistical Computer Performance Evaluation, ed. W. Freiberger, Academic Press, 1972, pp.465-484.

18. Littlewood, B., A Bayesian differential debugging model for software reliability. Proceedings of Workshop on Quantitative Software Models, 1979, pp. 170-81.

19. Musa, J.D., Iannino, A. and Okumoto, K., Software reliability measurement, prediction and application, McGraw-Hill, 1986.

20. Ball, A., Butterfield, M.H. and Dale, C.J., The achievement and assessment of safety in systems containing software. IAEA Specialists' Meeting on the use of Digital Computing Devices in Systems Important to Safety, Saclay, France, 28-29 November 1984.

21. Saglietti, F. and Ehrenberger, W., Software diversity - some considerations about its benefits and its limitations. IFAC SAFECOMP '86, Sarlat, France, 1986.

22. Saglietti, F. and Ehrenberger, W., Considerations on software diversity on the basis of experimental and theoretical work. ESPRIT '86: Results and Achievements, Directorate General XIII (editors), Elsevier Science Publishers B.V. (North-Hollaand), 1987.

23. Saglietti, F., A theoretical evaluation of the acceptance test as a means to achieve software fault-tolerance. IFIP/IFAC Working Conference on Hardware and Software for Real Time Process Control, Warsaw, 1988.

9

THE ROLE OF VERIFICATION AND VALIDATION

IN THE CERTIFICATION OF MILITARY AVIONIC SOFTWARE

ANDREW BRADLEY
British Aerospace Military Aircraft Division
Warton Aerodrome, Preston, PR4 1AX

ABSTRACT

Following an overview of the extent and role of digital systems in modern military aircraft a review of the certification process is given. Software aspects of the integrated systems approach are highlighted including hazard analysis and tracking, software classification, and the development activities which contribute to certification.

The roles of software Verification and Validation are discussed with particular emphasis on the effect of underlying expressional formality. The impact of formal specification methods on Verification and Validation activities at BAe Warton is described and the potential role of formal methods on the certification process is summarised.

INTRODUCTION

The wide BAe product range, spanning Civil Aircraft, Military Aircraft, Space & Communications and Dynamics Divisions, includes many examples of systems reliant upon software for correct operation. In many instances product attributes such as performance, defect rate, reliability and loss rate are guaranteed or certified as part of a contractual arrangement. BAe has wide experience thereby of the certification of products or systems containing software. This paper presents some aspects of such experience gained over recent years at Military Aircraft Division, Warton, illustrating product certification by the Experimental Aircraft Programme (EAP), homing in on software certification for that aircraft and concentrating particularly on software verification and validation. Recent developments in mathematically formal software techniques are described together with their impact on verification and validation and thereby the software certification process.

The relationship between aircraft certification, system certficiation and software certification must be clarified from the outset. They are all regarded as 'instances' of the more general concept of "product certification", the proposed definition of which is "declaration by an appropriate authority that the product design is proven as fit for its intended use". Hence either an aircraft, a system or a piece of software could be offered for certificaiton as a product and the same principles would apply. It is the plan of this paper firstly to illustrate the common principles by an example of aircraft certification (EAP). This enables digital systems design and certification to be put into context and, by analogy, sets the scene for a discussion of software certification. Some key aspects of activities supporting software certification are picked out, not least amongst which are Verification and Validation (V & V). After these introductory sections the bulk of this paper explores the impact of mathematical formality on V & V and comprises two main sub-sections. The first presents experience gained on EAP of developing and using a 'first generation' software development environment based on structured, semi-formal techniques. V & V activities are highlighted. The second presents the results of recent work to integrate mathematically formal specification and analysis techniques into the established, first generation approach. The impact of mathematical formality on V & V activities is described. The impact of formality on the overall certification process is summarised in the final section of the paper.

THE CERTIFICATION OF EAP

In this section we describe briefly the certification for flight of one product - EAP - in order to illustrate the general principles of product certification and to put into context the software certification related activities described later.

Digital Avionic Systems on EAP

EAP is a multi-national European project established to demonstrate the integration of advanced technologies needed to meet the demanding performance requirements of the next generation of fighter aircraft. The advanced technologies demonstrated range from the plainly visible structural aspects of components wholly made in carbon fibre to the invisible software necessary to navigate and automatically monitor and control the aircraft safely. The advanced, digital systems embedded in EAP include:

- Multi function displays and controls in an all electronic cockpit
- Fly-by-wire, full authority flight control system
- Utility systems management system (USMS - covering fuel gauging, hydraulics, etc.)

These systems are integrated into an overall aircraft system and communicate via MIL-STD-1553 serial data highways. The flight control system (FCS) comprises quadruplex hardware channels each running identical software on a RISC processor which was developed specifically for FCS application. A specialised technique [1] had already been developed to support the production of FCS software for the Jaguar Fly-by-Wire project and was used again on EAP. The avionics system and USMS software were produced primarily at BAe Warton using the lifecycle methods and tools described later in the paper (for a detailed description see [2]).

The Aircraft Certification Process

BAe's leading role in the certification for flight of EAP [3] is used here to illustrate the key elements and general principles of the certification process. In this 'aircraft' context the general definition of certification proposed above is instantiated as "a declaration by an appropriate authority that an aircraft design is proven as fit for flight". Building upon this definition the following key elements of the certification process emerge

- The existence of a certificating authority

- A set of criteria of fitness for flight, acceptable to the certificating authority

- An aircraft design

- An assessment of that design against the criteria by the certificating authority

- A conclusion by the authority that the design has been proven (or not) against the criteria.

To these key elements must be added organisations to procure the design from those who perform the design, a specification for the design and some feedback loops. Thereby the key elements are developed into general principles of the certification process as applied to an aircraft - see Figure 1.

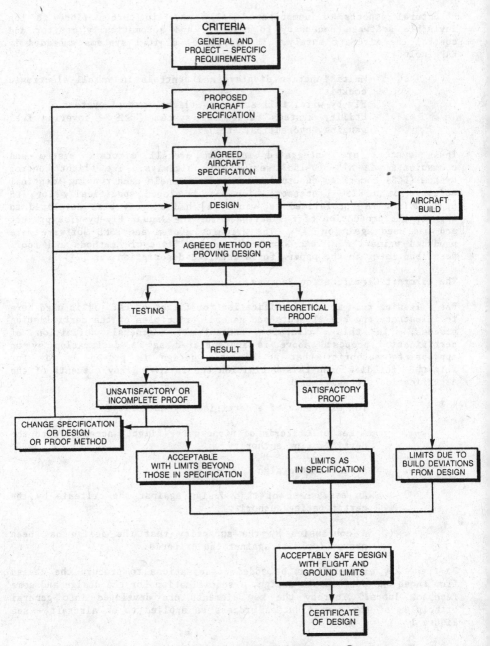

Fig.1 General Principles of Flight Certification Process

A certificating authority must ensure that there are suitable safety related criteria against which to assess fitness for flight. A customer organisation, having identified a need for an aircraft design, engages the services of a design organisation to provide one. The customer organisation proposes an aircraft specification consisting of fitness for flight requirements (the safety criteria against which the design will ultimately be assessed) and fitness for purpose requirements. The specification is agreed between customer, provider and certificating authority, and design commences.

The design is subjected to the agreed assessment methods to prove it meets the requirements. These methods may include physical testing, theoretical analysis and comparisons with proven existing designs. An unsatisfactory or incomplete result may be acceptable if limits (e.g. flight envelope restrictions) additional to those in the specification are imposed, or it may lead to a change to the specification, design or proof method. A satisfactory result is combined with any limitations from build to comprise evidence of proof of design. All evidence is assessed by the certificating authority for approval and certification.

The certification procedure developed and used for EAP was based upon this general process. The aircraft design was multi-national but it was offered for certification by BAe with MoD acting as a military airworthiness authority.

Figure 2 outlines the proof of design procedure used on EAP. The overall aircraft specification, containing fitness for flight requirements, is decomposed into system specifications containing system flight safety criteria. Each system design is assessed against its criteria leading to a proof of system design. A route map document, detailing all relevant system requirements and descriptions of assessment methods (tests, analyses, etc.), is produced for each system. System statements of design are ultimately produced, summarising all design evidence in a manner permitting requirements and evidence to be linked.

In many cases system specifications are further decomposed into equipment specifications. Individual equipments are subjected to the same assessment procedures leading, in the case of supplier provided equipments, to equipment certificates of design contributing to the higher level system design statements.

All system and equipment statements are collected together to form an aircraft statement of design, a concise record of design data and evidence of proof of design in support of the certification of the aircraft.

The Software Certification Process

The hierarchical relationship between aircraft, systems and equipments provides the framework for relating software certification to aircraft certification . It must be reiterated that aircaft certification and software certification are both instances of a common, general process. When an aircraft is offered for certification therefore, the process of software (and system ....) certification is effectively subsumed into the higher level activity. Through the hierarchy, however, software activities which contribute to aircraft certification can be identified and shown to conform to the general model of certification.

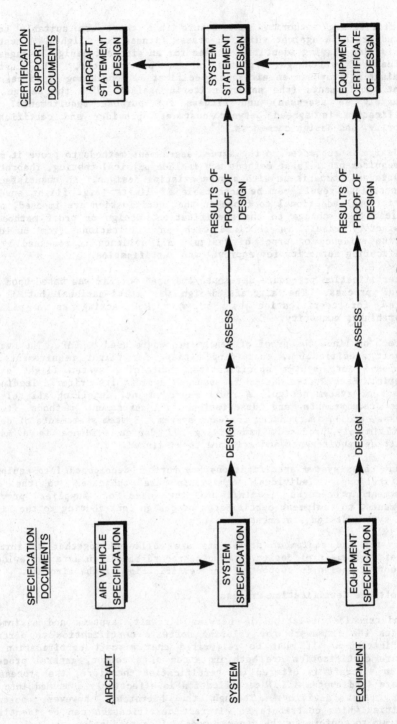

Fig.2 EAP – Outline of the Proof of Design Procedure

On EAP, software requirements and equipment specifications were derived from the system requirements/specifications described above. Software functional requirements were developed using CORE, a structured, tool supported methodology described in detail below (see Fig 3). Non functional, and in particular safety requirements, were developed by a process of system safety assessment, identifying hazards and analysing them against the proposed system design.

The hazard analyses were continued down through the functional requirements to software requirement level and resulted in a safety classification being derived for each software function. (safety critical, mission critical or non-critical). EAP experience proved that correct classification is vital since retrospective 'upgrading' is at best costly and more usually impractical. The extent and complexity of safety related software based functions is ever increasing due to increasing levels of systems integration and inter-dependence. A detailed discussion of this crucial area is beyond the scope of this paper however it is worth noting that few if any guidelines or standards give adequate consideration.

The functional requirements developed in CORE and the safety requirements derived as a classification constitute two principal criteria of software 'fitness for purpose'. These criteria form one of the key elements of the certification process.

Analagous to the next key element - aircraft design and build - is the software design and build, the EAP procedures for which are briefly described in the next section (see [2] for details). The analogy can be further extended by considering the assessment of the software design and build against the software requirements. At this stage in the software certification process, as in the aircaft process, agreed methods of proof are applied to the design in an attempt to show that it fulfills the stated requirements. In fact, since software design and build is a multi-phase process (Fig 3), both design and proof progress concurrently. Techniques, standards and practices appropriate to the established safety classifications are applied in both the production (i.e. design and build) and proof processes. The techniques, standards and practices for each class are agreed as being appropriate with both customer and certificating authority.

The analogy with aircaft certification is now almost complete. The provision of documentary evidence of the application of agreed techniques, standards and practices and of the results of all proof activities will allow assessment by the certificating authority that software requirements, both functional and non-functional, have been met.

The Role of Verification and Validation

It is generally accepted that, due primarily to the inherent complexity of software in typical embedded computer systems, the proof of design referred to above cannot be achieved solely by testing. Because of this there has been a shift in emphasis from product assessment to produciton process assessment. Hence produciton methods, tools, techniques and procedures, applied and enforced to pre-defined standards, have been employed in order to increase confidence in software products.

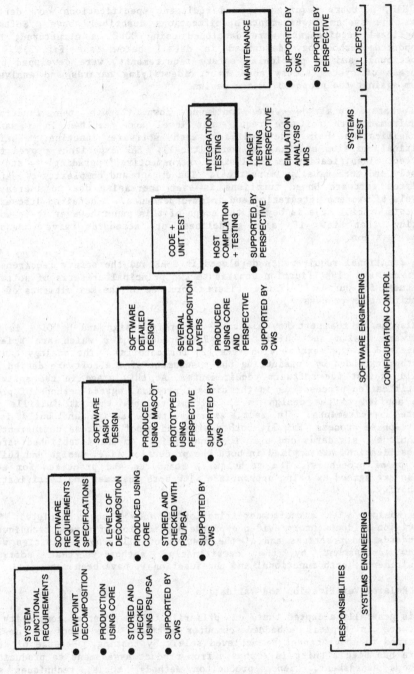

Figure 3 EAP SAFRA Lifecycle

The emergence of mathematically formal foundations for programming languages (e.g. [4]) and particularly specification 'languages' has brought the real possibility that software 'design and build' can be proven against software requirements by analysis. Although there are clear limitations conerning non-functional requirements, this possiblity if realised will contribute significantly to the certification process described above. The role of V&V in the general proof process is now outlined.

A 'traditional definition of verification is adopted:

> "the process of establishing that software satisfies its requirements" (RTCA-DO-178A).

It is common practice to apply the definition more 'locally' as a process of establishing that a representation at some level (e.g. detailed design) of the phased development cycle satisfies its requirements at the next higher level (e.g. basic design). 'Formal Verification' will be taken to mean a mathematically well founded verification method.

A quite restricted definition of validation is used:

> "the process of establishing that each representation is sound, complete and internally consistent".

'Formal Validation' will be taken to mean a mathematically well founded validation method. The more traditional definition of validation - "the process of establishing that the product, of which the software is a part, complies with equipment, system or aircraft level requirements" (RTCA-DO-178A) is often quoted. Within the hierarchical certification model developed above, however, this definition more aptly describes equipment, system or aircraft level verification.

With these definitions established it is clear that verification and validation by whatever means (analysis, testing, review,....) are prime constituents of the 'proof' method in the software certification process. The mathematically formal underpinning of these activities is therefore particularly important and forms the basis of the remainder of this paper.

In the next section we trace the BAe Warton history of adopting increasing levels of formality within the software development process. This will cover experience gained with 'first generation' structured techniques and the V&V activities which they enabled. This experience forms a sound basis for the introduction of mathematically formal techniqes and a proposed scheme for the synthesis of formal and structured techniques will be described. Within the resulting framework mathematically formal verification and validation can be established yielding the real possibility of 'proof by analysis' for critical software components.

THE IMPACT OF FORMALITY ON VERIFICATION AND VALIDATION

The realisation, over a decade ago, that the proliferation of embedded system software must be matched by increasing productivity levels has provided continuous motivation for BAe Warton to appraise, adopt and evolve effective software development techniques. The cost leverage inherent in an ability to eliminate errors early in the software lifecycle, using more formal methods of expression, led to an approach entitled Semi-Automated Functional Requirements Analysis (SAFRA). This approach was matured and proven on the EAP project and is now regarded as a 1st generation approach, the benefits of which have been clearly established and quantified. Over recent years the general development of languages and environments has combined with enhancements to SAFRA to evolve a 2nd generation approach, currently being transferred onto projects such as the European Fighter Aircraft (EFA). Increasing the levels of expressional formality used in requirements analysis and specification is one area of development which has been partially implemented in the 2nd generation approach and which will fundamentally underpin advanced 3rd generation techniques such as rapid prototyping, animation and large scale re-use [5].

In this section the SAFRA techniques are outlined highlighting the use of CORE (Controlled Requirements Expression) and the Verification and Validation techniques which were employed within this structured approach. The impact that mathematically formal specification and proof techniques will have on Verification and Validation activities on future projects is described within the context of FORMAL CORE, a BAe Warton development combining the strengths of both structured and formal methods.

The Impact of Structured Methods

SAFRA

The philosophy adopted for SAFRA was that each phase of the software lifecycle must be supported by a method and that each method or technique is supported by a corresponding tool. The methods and tools used to develop the EAP software are shown in Figure 3. Since BAe was essentially its own customer on this project no external functional requirement or specifications existed. Systems Engineering departments produced functional requirements and software specifications. There was then an interface to Software Engineering departments who embodied those requirements through basic and detailed design into code. Where no methods or tools existed new ones were developed. In particular, considerable development was undertaken to produce CORE, supported by a workstation. CORE embraces the lifecycle from functional requirements through to the production of detailed designs. On the other hand, where suitable tools were known to exist, they were imported and integrated.

CORE

CORE is a method of expressing and analysing requirements in a controlled, structured and primarily diagrammatic manner. The method comprises 11 logical steps which when applied to a requirement will decompose it into lower level components to which, in turn, the method can be applied. The 11 steps are listed and a complete description and comparison with other techniques given in Ref. [6]

Those concepts most relevant to the subsequent discussion on formal methods are picked out and briefly described here.

When capturing the requirements of a system two types of <u>viewpoint</u> re used. Firstly the direct, external influences on the system (e.g. users, other systems, ...) are grouped into 3 or 4 'bounding viewpoints'. (Figure 4). For each such viewpoint, and for the system itself (also treated as a viewpoint) a <u>'tabular entry'</u> is created, comprising a list of high level actions performed by the viewpoint. Each action is annotated with high level or abstract data items consumed and produced, together with their source and destination viewpoints. In this way information is gathered about the system, its environment and information flow across the system boundary. Secondly the system itself is decomposed or partitioned by identifying 3 or 4 'defining viewpoints' within it. This process continues hierarchically, each viewpoint being split into 3 or 4 further viewpoints, so that a viewpoint tree structure is created within which requirements can be expressed and reconciled. This corresponds to the hierarchical aircraft/systems/equipments structure developed earlier in the discussion of the certification process. (Figure 5). Working down the tree tabular entries are created for each viewpoint, thus gathering information about the functions of the system in a logical and controlled manner. Information flow between viewpoints at the same level is checked for consistency and, where appropriate, <u>data decomposition</u> diagrams are provided to display the internal structure of abstract or high level data items. Final stages of viewpoint selection may involve identification of hardware sub systems or components.

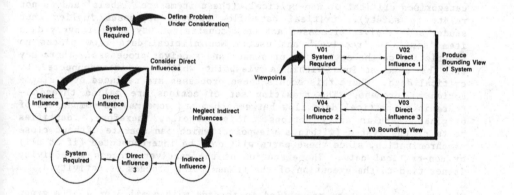

Figure 4   Bounding Viewpoints in Core

Viewpoint selection, at any level, stimulates the creation of tabular entries – lists of actions which each viewpoint performs – at an appropriate level of detail. Subsequent steps in the method investigate relationships between and ultimately modify these actions, both within and across viewpoints.

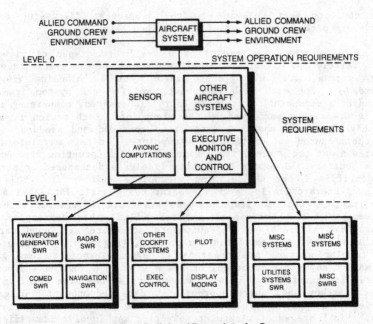

ALLIED COMMAND
GROUND CREW
ENVIRONMENT

AIRCRAFT
SYSTEM

ALLIED COMMAND
GROUND CREW
ENVIRONMENT

LEVEL 0   SYSTEM OPERATION REQUIREMENTS

SENSOR

OTHER
AIRCRAFT
SYSTEMS

SYSTEM
REQUIREMENTS

AVIONIC
COMPUTATIONS

EXECUTIVE
MONITOR
AND
CONTROL

LEVEL 1

WAVEFORM
GENERATOR
SWR

RADAR
SWR

OTHER
COCKPIT
SYSTEMS

PILOT

MISC
SYSTEMS

MISC
SYSTEMS

COMED
SWR

NAVIGATION
SWR

EXEC
CONTROL

DISPLAY
MODING

UTILITIES
SYSTEMS
SWR

MISC
SWRS

Figure 5   Defining Viewpoints in Core

Within a viewpoint every data item in the tabular entry is considered and
categorised critical or non-critical. (these items are 'labels' and do not
relate to safety).   Critical data flow between processes implies that
sender and receiver processes act in a constrained way so that every data
item 'sent' is 'received' and used.   Non critical data flow places no
restriction on the activation of sender and receiver processes.   There may
then be some actions within a viewpoint which are interconnected by
critical data.   Where this occurs these processes are replaced by a single
action or process.   The resulting set of actions are called <u>threads</u> -
there is no critical data flow between them and some may be composites of
original, tabular entry actions.   This exercise, therefore, identifies
parts of the system (within a viewpoint) which can operate without close
synchronisation, since these parts will only be interconnected (if at all)
by non-critical data.   The execution of the receiver process or activity
is not tied to the execution of the transmitting process or activity.

When actions have been reconciled to threads within all 3 or 4 of a group
of viewpoints the exercise is generalised to identify 'threads of threads'
(<u>combined threads</u>) comprising threads within different viewpoints linked
by critical data flow across viewpoint boundaries.   (Figure 6).   This
activity pin-points areas of functionality in the system which require to
be closely coupled by buffers, queues or interleaving execution, and where
data are preserved as they flow from one activity to another.

Within CORE the functional behaviour of processes is specified using a
combination of two techniques, graphical and algorithmic.   The graphical
notation extends the basic 'box and line' format with additional symbols
and constructs encompassing box decomposition, iteration, mutual exclusion
and functional equivalence.

Match and Draw Combined Threads

Consider the Data Flow Between Threads Across All Viewpoints

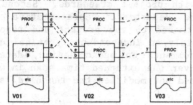

Consider the Nature of the Data Across the Viewpoint Boundary, Look for
Synchronisation Between Processes, ie 'Critical' Data Flow

Draw Combined Threads

Draw the Synchronised Isolated Threads in Temporal Order

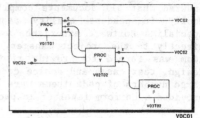

Figure 6   Combined Threads in Core

Each diagram box is also supported by a 'structured design note' wherein
algorithmic relationships between process input, output and local data
items is recorded. The algorithmic notation may be a descriptive
narrative at high abstract levels of the viewpoint tree or it may be a
detailed, pseudo-code representation of a function at low levels of the
tree. This combination of diagrammatic layering and algorithmic notations
is used to specify requirements at a detailed level, within a framework of
viewpoints and threads which encapsulates requirements for
synchronisation, coupling and temporal interactions of the basic processes
or actions.

Whilst there are a number of additional aspects of the CORE, 11 step
method which cannot adequately be detailed here, the points more relevant
to subsequent discussion have been highlighted. In summary CORE is a
structured method within a primarily diagrammatic notation. When applied
to real-time control systems and their environments it facilitates and
supports the capture of functional requirements, the definition of
software requirements and the decomposition of the overall software
function into loosely coupled processes.

Verification and Validation

A major objective of the EAP software development project was to improve
the quality of the delivered software by the production of clear,
unambiguous and complete requirement specifications. It was recognised
that software quality cannot inherently be introduced into the delivered
product by testing and therefore, in establishing the project, two thrusts
for quality were defined and applied. First, 'built-in' quality was
planned for by the application of CORE to ensure consistency and
completeness of the requirements and subsequent documents. Secondly,
analysis and review of documents produced for each phase of the lifecycle
allowed the quality of the product to be evaluated and corrective action
to be taken where necessary to rectify any deficiencies.

The software standards and procedures stated how quality control would be
achieved for each phase and laid down the verification and validation
procedures for document analysis, technical audit, review and testing. To
ensure compliance with the standards and adherence to procedures three
responsibilities were identified.

Firstly, a project quality controller ensured that all automated CORE analysis checks were completed prior to document reviews and generally ensured that all documents complied with project standards. Secondly a wholly independent quality assurance department representative with specialist software experience was seconded to the project and reported directly to the project manager. Thirdly an independent technical audit team was formed to provide review comments on basic design, detailed design, test cases and source code. Over the extended time span in which large numbers of code items were created and modified the technical audit provided a uniform level of inspection.

The manual methods employed by the technical audit team reflect strongly the capabilities of currently available verification and validation tools such as SPADE [7]. Firstly, for non-trivial items a directed graph control flow representation was constructed and assessed for deficiencies such as unreachable code and non-exitable loops. Secondly various data flow and definition checks were applied to the process for example ensuring that all output data items are defined on each path through the control flow graph. Thirdly a manual compliance analysis was performed by constructing a 'truth table' representation of the developed design or code and analysing this representation against the higher level specification. Fourthly test plans were assessed against code with the aim of ensuring that pre-defined coverage requirements had been met.

In summary the use of CORE as the backbone of the development process provided a continuity of notation and method which facilitated comprehensive verification and validation activities at all levels. Validation within levels was achieved by automated consistency and completeness checking within the CORE databases, an independent technical audit team applying manual static analysis techniques covering control and data flow and finally traditional testing. Verification from level to level was achieved by a combination of CORE automated checking, testing, traditional review and manual compliance analysis.

The Impact of Formal Methods

Formal Methods

Steadily over a number of years, and prolifically over recent years, new methods of software specification and development based on pure mathematics have been emerging from academic and industrial institutions. The motivation for employing mathematically formal notations and methods in the specification and development of software is identical to the motivation for employing structured methods such as CORE, namely the removal of errors early in the production process both to improve the quality of delivered software and to increase the productivity of software engineers.

The term 'formal method' is widely used in varying contexts. Hence we list the principal aspects or components of a formal method as discussed in this paper.

- A mathematical notation and set of rules

- A specification structuring method

- A 'formal validation' method of proving completeness and self consistency of specification

- A method of 'refinement' whereby an abstract specification is transformed or reified into a programming language implementation

- A 'formal verification' method of proof of refinement steps

The branches of mathematics which are common to most of the notations and methods developed so far are

-	Logic and predicate calculus	- as an enhancement of Boolean operators, types and rules common to many programming languages.
-	Set theory	- as a method of specifying operations on collections of data in a manner which is independent of the method of storage of the data in a computer.

The key to effective use of these branches of mathematics is abstraction - i.e. the statement of a requirement in a form which is independent of the notations and restrictions of any software implementation language, the use of a 'problem notation' rather than a 'solution notation'.

In addition to improving the quality and precision of specifications, formal methods offer the prospect of combining with programming languages, proven to be mathematically self-consistent and well defined, to allow mathematical proof that a 'solution' embodied in a programme satisfies a requirement stated in a formal specification notation. i.e. the 'proof' step in the certification process described above. Whilst currently feasible only for small systems, the prospect of proving an implementation of a safety critical function against a clear, precise and concise specification is a strong motivation for active involvement in this field. The increasing adoption of computer hardware in safety critical avionic systems has generated such involvement at BAe Warton.

It is not possible here to give a comprehensive overview of the formal methods field, rather we concentrate on what is widely regarded as the most mature class of methods - the model based specification techniques, of which the Vienna Development Method (VDM [8] and Z [9]) are the most extensively used in industry.

The model based techniques have a common structure which involves the definition of a 'state' to model the internal structure (or memory) of the system. (Figure 7). The state is modelled as abstractly as possible using mathematical sets or higher level objects such as sequences and mappings. The aim is to encapsulate essential features of the system without introducing unnecessary implementation details. Operations are defined which may depend upon and affect the values of the state components and may also depend upon 'external' input variables and may generate 'external' output variables. This structure is common to all types of applications, from transaction processing and database systems to plant control and monitoring.

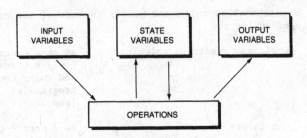

Figure 7   Basic Format of Model Based Formal Specification Methods

After detailed appraisal, Z was selected as the subject of an extensive programme of work aimed at investigating its relationship to and possible integration with the CORE based SAFRA methodology. Z is a product of the Programming Research Group at Oxford University and comprises a primarily set-theoretic notation extended to define relations, functions, sequences, etc. and associated operators. Data typing in terms of these entities is complemented by propositional and predicate calculus to yield a notation which is expressive and extendible.

Particular strengths of Z are its structuring facilities and its presentational clarity. Structuring is provided by a 'schema' notation (Figure 8) whereby a complete specification is constructed by defining and combining a number of schema operations, each representing some partial aspect of the overall requirements. A Z schema comprises two parts:

°   the signature   -   a declaration of the names and types of variables involved in the operation.

°   the predicate   -   a mathematically stated relationship between the elements of the signature.

The predicate may take the form of an explicit 'pre-condition' a statement which must be satisfied for the operation to be invoked and an explicit 'post-condition' a statement describing the effect of the operation. Presentational clarity derives partially from the schema structuring and partially from the interspersion of descriptive, narrative text, used to complement the mathematical formality and render the specification 'readable', even by those unfamiliar with Z.

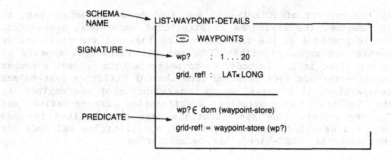

SCHEMA NAME → LIST-WAYPOINT-DETAILS

⊜ WAYPOINTS

SIGNATURE →

wp?   : 1 ... 20

grid. ref! : LAT× LONG

PREDICATE →

wp? ∈ dom (waypoint-store)

grid-ref! = waypoint-store (wp?)

Figure 8   A Z Schema

Whilst enjoying increasing use in industry the Z notation and method are not rigorously standardised nor adequately supported by tools. There are also strict limits to the scope of applicability of the method, especially in the area of real-time control systems. Large scale structuring, process synchronisations and temporal aspects in general are not supported.

In summary formal methods offer a further increase in expressional formality beyond that already achieved by the adoption of structured methods such as CORE. The model based or 'constructive' class of methods is the most established and widely used. Z was selected by BAe Warton for detailed evaluation and possible integration with CORE.

<u>Formal CORE</u>

It is clear from the previous two sections that the strengths of CORE may be complemented by those of formal methods in the application domain of large, real-time avionic systems.

CORE is a powerful, structured method for the controlled and modular development of system requirements and specifications with particular emphasis on module interaction synchronisations and temporal relationships. Mathematical formalisation of the temporal interactions of processes is still a research area, however the loosely coupled processes defined by CORE analysis are potentially amenable to established formal methods. On EAP the functional content of CORE threads was specified informally (descriptive narrative) high in the viewpoint hierarchy (i.e. early in the lifecycle) and semi-formally (diagrammatic decomposition and pseudo-code) later in the lifecycle. The use of Z allows precise, formal definition early in the lifecycle followed by potentially verifiable refinement thereafter.

In this way the concept of FORMAL CORE was evolved as an enhancement to SAFRA which combines the strengths of structured and formal approaches. An interface is proposed at the thread level so that all temporal aspects of requirements are captured within CORE and all functional aspects of threads are specified in Z. In order to investigate this concept a number of representative threads were selected from the EAP Utilities Systems and formally re-specified in Z, based on an understanding of the engineering requirements (gained from existing specification documentation and interviewing engineers). The specifications were then refined to code (PASCAL) before a detailed comparison of both specification and code was made with the original, CORE-based, EAP documentation.

Although the Utilities Systems threads chosen for study were quite small (<100 lines code when implemented) clear indications of the benefits of formality were seen. These prompted further study in the form of a relatively large (2000 lines of code) case study which had proved particularly difficult to specify and design using standard CORE – namely Soft-Key decoding for the multi-function displays in the all electronic cockpit of EAP. Combining the results and conclusions from this series of initial case studies the following main points emerged:

- the strengths of the formal notation and method (precision, clarity, verifiability and specification by construction) complement the strengths of the CORE semi-formal notation and method (organised requirements capture, techniques for handling dynamics, temporal aspects, concurrency)

- embedding formal methods in an established, structured approach is a viable way to feed formality from a research and development environment through to projects

- the formal definitions of a domain vocabularly – i.e. a set of formally defined functions which are specific to the application and used frequently – helps to conceal unnecessary detail in specifications and provides a natural working language for systems engineers.

- in all the case studies the use of the formal method resulted in enhanced clarity, visibility and traceability (therefore vastly improving the prospects of effective software maintenance). Also, notably these benefits were not at the expense of code size, performance, ... but in fact were accompanied by a reduction in code size together with reduced stack usage.

- more effort is expended on requirements capture/specification when a formal notation and method is employed. Less effort is expended on design and coding – the refinement from specification to code being relatively straightforward for avionic systems which are not dominated by complex data structures.

- there is a marked lack of mature tool support for creating, analysing and refining formal specifications.

there is a barrier, at best only perceived but probably real, on the part of software (and more so systems) engineers to the introduction of mathematical techniques into the software production process.

In addition it was established that the formal notation enables extensive formal analysis of safety critical system specifications to be performed and that formal specifications are pre-requisites for the application of automated code analysis tools. Since a total verification scheme for safety critical avionic software is a prime goal of research at BAe Warton we expand here on the verification and validation aspects of the case study findings.

Formal Verification and Validation

Static analysis tools form a key element in the BAe WARTON approach to the formal verification and validation of high integrity software. Over the past 2 years evaluation of the SPADE suite of tools has been performed in two phases.

Following acquisition and familiarisation the first phase involved application of SPADE to sections of ADA code taken from a Flight Control System. Considering separately the flow analysis tools (those which address intrinsic properties of the code - validation) and the sematic analysis tools (those which address compliance of the code with its specification - verification) it was found that the former were straightforward to apply and extremely effective (for detailed information on the flow analysis tools see [7]). The effectiveness of the sematic analysis however was limited by the lack of detailed formal specifications, relying instead on the analysts knowledge of the desired function of the code. The second phase evaluation of SPADE was based on the FORMAL CORE case studies and used the formal specifications to evaluate fully the semantic analysis tools. Clearly the SPADE and FORMAL CORE developments are complementary. Their successful integration is intended to provide a complete verification and validation scheme for processes within avionic software systems.

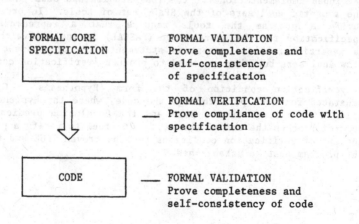

Formal validation of CORE threads, functionally specified in Z, is achieved methodically by an analysis process similar to that described by Wordsworth [10], extended for application to real-time control systems. The functional specification in Z respects the input and output data interfaces of the CORE thread. These interfaces may comprise low-level signal/data definitions or more abstract data types. The method encourages the production of complete, concise and self-consistent specifications:

complete –	the input and state data space is spanned completely by the operations
concise –	the notation is precise, economical and directed toward the application domain wherever possible
consistent –	all operations are mutually consistent in effect in areas of the input and state data space where they 'overlap'.

The starting point for the analysis is a set of 'partial' operations together with the 'state' model and any global invariants or relationships. In the production of this initial set of functional requirements no attempt is made to compose or impose a 'top down' structure. In this way, individual operations or small groups of operations are likely to be defined in terms of engineering requirements rather than computing (control flow, target language, ...) requirements. The analysis and extension of the partial operations proceeds by making explicit within operations all pre-conditions which ensure that state invariants are maintained. The attributes of completeness and self-consistency are established via a partitioning process which is also aimed at producing a logically optimised structure for the specification which can be carried forward to design and code.

The relationship between the formally validated specifications and the developed implementations of the case studies has been investigated using the semantic analysers of the SPADE set of tools. In order to formally verify a program the tools require that a representation of the specification for the source code (PASCAL) is included within the source as assertions. These assertion statements are transparent to the SPADE flow analysers but they are used to produce 'verification conditions'.

A verification condition of the form 'Hypothesis   Conclusion' is generated for each path through the code, where the Hypothesis predicate holds at the start of the path and the Conclusion predicate holds when control reaches the end of the path. In order to verify a program each of the set of verification conditions must be proven TRUE and termination of the program must be established.

It was concluded from the case studies that formal verification of PASCAL against Z specifications was a straightforward but time-consuming task. The structural simplicity of the code, which was a reflection of the validation work performed on the specification, meant that flow analysis messages were few and that the verification conditions were manageable. It is essential that code is developed in an analysable language subset (be it PASCAL, ADA, ASSEMBLER, ...) since it is difficult if not impractical to convert to a subset for analysis purposes. Furthermore the use of proof assistance tools is regarded as essential for the methods to be practicable on project.

In summary, recent advances in the capabilities of tools such as SPADE, enabling formal proof of program compliance with mathematically formal specifications, are expected to have significant impact on established software verification practices. The developments are complementary to the formal validation aspects of BAe's FORMAL CORE and both will contribute to an overall software verification and validation procedure.

SUMMARY

In this paper we have highlighted verification and validation as important activities which contribute to software certification. We have attempted both to put software certification into context and to describe recent industry developments which will contribute significantly to the software certification process.

The general process of product certification was developed and illustrated by an example of aircraft certification - EAP. Because of the extensive deployment of embedded computer systems on EAP, this example allowed us to put software certification into a systems and aircraft hierarchical context, at the same time illustrating how software certification conforms to the general product model. Software verification and validation were identified as key elements in the 'proof of design' activity within the certification process.

Drawing upon EAP experience as a common thread in this paper, verification and validation were described within a 'first generation' software engineering approach based on the CORE structured method. As has now become commonplace, assessment of the production process, as well as the product, played a significant role in the overall 'proof of design' activity. The impact of mathematically formal methods on software verification and validation was then explored. BAe developments combining formal methods with CORE, together with the emergence of mathematically based code analysis tools have combined to yield a mathematically formal verification and validaiton scheme offering the prospect of 'proof of design' by analysis. The adoption of these technques on project is being vigorously pursued at BAe Warton.

REFERENCES

1. Daley, E. and Smith, R.B., Flight clearance of the Jaguar Fly-by-Wire. Certification of Avionic Systems, Royal Aeronautical Society, London, England, April 1982.

2. Cronshaw, P., The Experimental Aircraft Programme software toolset. Software Engineering Journal, November 1986, 236-247.

3. Bradshaw, W., Certification of Advanced Experimental Aircraft. International Council of the Aeronautical Sciences, 15th Congress London, 1986.

4. Carre, B.A. and Jennings, T., SPARK - The SPADE ADA Kernel, An Outline of the Language. University of Southampton.

5. Ward, A.O., Three generations of software engineering for airborne systems. Software Engineering and its application to avionics. Advisory Group on Aeronautical Research and Development Proceedings, 1988, to be published.

6. Looney, M., CORE-STARTS debrief report, 1986, National Computing Centre, Manchester, England.

7. Carre, B.A., Clutterbuck, D.L., Debney C.W., O'Neill, I.M., SPADE - the Southampton Program Analysis and Development Environment, in Software Engineering Environments, IEE computing Series 7, Peter Perigrinus Ltd.

8. Jones, C.B., Systematic software development using VDM. 1986. Prentice Hall International Series in Computer Science.

9. Hayes, I., Specification case studies. 1987. Prentice Hall International Series in Computer Science.

10. Wordsworth, J., A Z Development Method. Internal report, IBM UK Ltd, Mail Point 149, Hursley, England.

10

THE ROLE OF STATISTICAL MODELING AND INFERENCE IN SOFTWARE QUALITY ASSURANCE

DOUGLAS R. MILLER
Department of Operations Research
School of Engineering and Applied Science
George Washington University
Washington, DC 20052

ABSTRACT

In order to assure software quality, we would like to take a traditional statistical approach. This involves collecting data and using a model to make statistical inferences about software reliability. In particular, we try to infer that the software meets a required level of reliability. In critical applications where extremely reliable software is required, it may be impossible to assure the reliability in a statistically rigorous way. However, there are other important roles for statistical methods in attempting to assure software quality.

INTRODUCTION

Software quality assurance can be very important. It can make the difference between life and death. Software controlling life-critical systems may not perform as desired, resulting in catastrophic consequences. The goal of software quality assurance methodologies is to prevent such undesirable events. The certification of software reflects confidence that occurrence rates of such events will be less than some very low, socially accepntable rate; or it may even reflect confidence that such bad events are impossible. The activities of software assurance and software certification merit close scrutiny. A critical scientific investigation should be performed. This paper may contribute to such an investigation.

It is important to distinguish among achievement, assessment, and assurance of software quality. When a piece of software is put in service to perform some function, it may or may not perform as desired. If it has been carefully and skillfully developed, it will probably work as desired most of the time; however, it may occasionally not perform as required. We are concerned about the occurrence of software failure events. Attaining an acceptable rate of occurrence is an achievement. Achievement of software quality can be obtained by using good software development methods; or possibly by a combination of poor methods, clever people and luck. Software quality <u>assessment</u> is the measurement of quality, or verification that a desired level of achievement has been attained. Software quality can be assessed by observing its performance. The <u>assurance</u> of software quality refers to a *priori* confidence in the achievement of quality. It is usually necessary to have a *priori* confidence for software controlling life-critical systems. Society requires certification of certain software prior to public use; the certification should be interpreted as a statement of assurance. Assurance, as defined above, is the subject of this paper.

Software quality assurance can be approached in different ways. A major distinction is "qualitative" versus "quantitative." The qualitative approach to assurance is based on using good software engineering practice, documentation of the development process, and scrutiny by impartial observers. Subjective evaluation of previous experiences with similar systems and engineering judgment are important aspects of this approach.

A quantitative approach to software quality assurance must be based on probability and statistics. This is because we are dealing with "uncertainty." The system may or may not perform as required during its lifetime. The uncertainty in performance includes possibilities of software errors and also incomplete knowledge of the usage environment of the software. It is unrealistic to believe a *prior* that a software system will function perfectly in all situations encountered during its lifetime. Some level of doubt must be admitted; the risk of undesirable events occurring exists. We want assurance that the risk is acceptable. The quantitative equivalent is confidence that the <u>probability</u> of failure is less than some acceptable level. The quantitative approach is based on the scientific method of observation, measurement and inference. Because we are trying to deal quantitatively with uncertainty, the inferences will be <u>statistical</u> inferences about probabilities.

With software in life-critical systems, acceptable probabilities of failure are usually extremely low. The FAA [6] advises that probabilities of loss of life should be less than 10^{-9} per mission for commercial aircraft. Thus a quantitative approach to software quality assurance leads to statistical analysis involving extremely low probabilities. A rigorous statistical solution is almost certainly impossible. Some reasons supporting this conclusion are given below.

Despite its limitations, statistical analysis can still play an important role in software quality assurance. It can be used in support of assurance in some cases. In other instances, it can be used to challenge claims of assurance based on qualitative judgments. Statistical analysis can generally be used to gain deeper understanding of software development and quality assurance phenomena.

THE STATISTICAL APPROACH TO ASSURANCE

The traditional statistical approach to dealing with uncertainty uses the scientific method originally proposed by Roger Bacon. The system or phenomenon under study is observed, measurements made and collected as data, and then inferences are made about the system. Observation of software systems could occur in the field, in a laboratory test bed, or even as a simulated emulation. The type of inferences to be made involve reliability and consequences of system failures.

In order to make inferences about real-world behavior from experimental data, there must be some link between the experiment and the real world. This requires making some assumptions. Depending on the situation, these assumptions might be straightforward, simple, and clear; or they might be complex and approximate. These assumptions constitute the statistical model. We shall consider various models, and note the absence of models for some situations.

Software testing and quality assurance encounter the above important aspect of modelling. If the software test is completely representative of real-world usage, then real-world behavior can be inferred from the behavior during testing. One way to get representative behavior is to base the test on a completely random selection from the real-world usage; this is random testing, which leads to a simple and useful model that we will use later to make inferences. In contrast, non-random testing, such as functional testing, does not represent real-world usage very closely. The relationship between software behavior under non-random testing and under real-world usage is not understood: no model exists. If a model is developed it would probably be complicated and approximate, so that any inferences based on it would also be approximate.

A general rule for statistical analysis is that "you don't get something for nothing." You can generally make stronger inferences from increased amounts of data. If a different model allows one to make stronger inferences based on less data, it probably means that the model is based on restrictive assumptions which favor the stronger inference. Validation of the model might require huge amounts of data.

One of the major problems with statistical analysis is the approximate nature of statistical models. If the domain of application concerns moderately small probabilities, like .01 or .001, or even .0001, then the models may ignore certain negligible factors or make small approximations; but in the realm of very small probabilities such as 10^{-9}, it seems unwise to make any approximations or assumptions. In the domain of ultrareliability, validation of models is probably impossible. Much software modelling is oriented toward a batch-processing environment; however, this is the wrong model for many situations, such as that of ultrareliable avionics software. Many difficult complications are encountered in the modelling and analysis of ultrareliable control software. Some of them are:

. extreme importance of interfaces and exception handling;

. the crucial role of compilers;

. "all the things you didn't think of;" and

. imperfect knowledge of the usage distribution.

Consideration of the first three of these problems raises the possibility that the software should be treated as a black box which must undergo incredibly tedious testing in order to verify high reliability, and that rigorous statistical verification of ultrareliability may be impossible.

When taking a statistical approach to assurance of very high software quality, it is important to be very critical and careful. Hidden or unstated assumptions must be exposed. The rest of this paper looks at these issues.

RELIABILITY GROWTH

Software reliability growth models appear to occupy a significant position in the statistical methodology for software assurance. Reliability growth models [11,17] have been used successfully in cases with moderate levels of reliability. For example, Currit, Dyer, and Mills [2] successfully use such models for a system in which they cite failure rates very roughly in the neighborhood of one failure per 5000 test cases. However, to achieve and assure ultrahigh levels of software reliability through reliability growth requires prohibitively long sequences of random testing. When reliability growth is achieved through functional testing (which might require less testing if the tester is incredibly astute), there is no way to make inferences about the real-world reliability of the debugged program.

Bev Littlewood [10] has made the following observation about the reliability growth rate for software for which data has been published: the current reliability as measured by interfailure times is at least an order of magnitude less than the total accumulated testing time. Thus to achieve interfailure times of one million hours, say, would require at least 10 million hours of random testing and debugging. Table 1 shows this phenomenon for one of Musa's [12] data sets.

Looking at reliability growth data in the above way leads one to make a general inference: to achieve long interfailure times in software which is initially unacceptable requires very long testing and debugging. This inference is based on very few assumptions; the main assumption is that testing is representative of real-world usage. For example, it is unnecessary to assume that successive test cases are independent.

The above conclusion addresses quality achievement; it does not provide assurance for a particular piece of software. It is a negative conclusion in the sense that it shows how bad the situation is. Such negative results provided by statistical analysis can prevent overly optimistic or unsupported claims of software quality.

TABLE 1

A Typical Data Set Showing Slow Reliability Growth

Failure Number	Cumulative Time	Interfailure Time	Ratios of Interfailure to Cumulative Time
.	.	.	.
.	.	.	.
.	.	.	.
110	49416	245	.0050
111	50145	729	.0145
112	52042	1897	.0365
113	52489	447	.0085
114	52875	386	.0073
115	53321	446	.0084
116	53443	122	.0023
117	54433	990	.0182
118	55381	948	.0171
119	56463	1082	.0192
120	56485	22	.0004
121	56560	75	.0013
122	57042	482	.0084
123	62551	5509	.0881
124	62651	100	.0016
125	62661	10	.0002
126	63732	1071	.0168
127	64103	371	.0058
128	64893	790	.0122
129	71043	6150	.0866
130	74364	3321	.0447
131	75409	1045	.0139
132	76057	648	.0085
133	81542	5485	.0673
134	82702	1160	.0140
135	84566	1864	.0220
136	88682	4116	.0464

ASSURING ULTRARELIABILITY OF SOFTWARE

Software used in real-time control of safety-critical systems must be ultrareliable. The software in digital flight control computers aboard commercial aircraft will be critical to flight safety. Reliability on the order of 10^{-9} failures per hour or per mission is desired. Even trying to quantify such high reliability with statistical parameter values is very difficult and may be meaningless. The Radio Technical Commission for Aeronautics refrained from quantifying the reliability; in "Software Considerations in Airborne Systems and Equipment Certification," DO-178A, [18], they say:

"During the preparation of this document, techniques for estimating the post-verification probabilities of software errors were examined. The objective was to develop numerical requirements for such probabilities for digital computer-based equipment and systems certification. The conclusion reached, however, was that currently available methods do not yield results in which confidence can be placed to the level required for this purpose. Accordingly, this document does not state post-verification software error requirements in these terms."

In Advisory Circular No. 25.1309-1, [6], the FAA uses the value 10^{-9} to characterize "extremely improbable." Such events would be unlikely to occur during the entire lifetime of a fleet of aircraft. To see some rationale for this number, consider the following rough calculation: A single plane with a 30-year lifetime flies approximately 10^4 days, at most 10 hours per day. So a fleet of 10^3 planes would accumulate at most 10^8 flight hours. We would expect 0.10 occurences of an event with 10^{-9} probability during this time. The Poisson distribution is a good model for such rare events; so the probability of no occurences is exp(-0.10) $= .90$, which is somewhat unlikely.

In theory, statistical verification of any level of reliability is possible. In practice, we encounter at least three major difficulties: the usage distribution used in testing may not perfectly fit the usage distribution encountered in the field; fixes may be imperfect; test time may be limited. The usage distribution is a severe problem: it may be desirable to bias the test distribution to go after bugs which the tester thinks are more likely to be in the software, but perfect knowledge of the field usage distribution is needed to remove this bias in estimating the reliability. The problem of imperfect fixes can be avoided by considering the software to be completely new after each fix and thus not trying to base inferences about failure rate on previous versions. Furthermore it is unlikely that bugs would be allowed to remain in the program after they have been detected, so each version would be tested until it fails; then it becomes a new version. So an estimate of reliability would be based on failure-free tests. In order to have any degree of confidence that the failure rate is less than 10^{-9} failures/hour, it is necessary to test for more than 10^9 hours and experience no failures.

Confidence intervals for failure probabilities based on error-free testing can be derived as follows. Let p denote the unknown probability of failure on a given randomly chosen test case. Suppose n test cases are run with no failure observed. In general, when n is large and p is small, the number of failures will be a random variable, X, with a Poisson distribution with mean $\mu = np$:

$$P(X = x) = e^{-\mu}\mu^x/x! , \quad x = 0, 1, 2, \ldots .$$

Thus we have observed data to which this model assigns probability

$$P(X = 0) = e^{-\mu} = e^{-np}.$$

The values of p for which these data are not statistically significant at level α are those satisfying

$$\alpha \leq P(X = 0) = e^{-np}$$

or

$$p \leq -\log\alpha/n ,$$

which constitutes a $100(1-\alpha)\%$ confidence interval for p, if n test cases are run without failure. For various confidence levels the confidence intervals are:

Estimation of p Based on 0 Failures in n Trials

Confidence Level	Confidence Interval
95%	$p < 3.00/n$
99%	$p < 4.61/n$
99.9%	$p < 6.91/n$
99.99%	$p < 9.21/n$
99.999%	$p < 11.51/n$

For example, to be 99% confident that the failure probability is less than 10^{-9} requires 4.6×10^9 test cases without failure. If the unit of time is hours, this equals 525,000 years. (A more simplistic approach of 10^9 failure free hours is still equal to 114,000 years of testing.) A side issue is that the software would have to be much more reliable than 10^{-9} in order to survive 4.6×10^9 test cases without failing. Thus, infeasibly long testing times are necessary to verify high reliability and they probably would not work anyway because knowing the real-world usage distribution precisely enough is a problem.

For the sake of argument, suppose we embark on the above type of heroic testing. Suppose one failure occurs in n trials. A confidence interval for p can also be found based on this data. Assuming the above Poisson model

$$P(X \leq 1) = e^{\mu}\mu^0/0! + e^{-\mu}\mu^1/1! = e^{-\mu}(1+\mu)$$

Solving the equation

$$\alpha = (1 + \mu_\alpha) \exp(-\mu_\alpha)$$

gives $\mu_{.05} = 4.74$, $\mu_{.01} = 6.64$, $\mu_{.0001} = 11.8$, etc. The confidence intervals for p are:

Estimation of p Based on 1 Failure in n Trials

Confidence Level	Confidence Interval
95%	$p < 4.74/n$
99%	$p < 6.64/n$
99.99%	$p < 11.8/n$

In practice, the design error which caused the failure would be corrected. This creates a new version. The quality assurance of the new version must start from scratch, because we do not have adequate models of successive versions of software. (Reliability growth models are adequate at nominal levels of reliability, but are unacceptable approximations at ultrahigh levels of reliability.)   Thus, it is much safer to base reliability estimates on failure-free test data.

The above analysis can be used incorrectly. Suppose the software is tested for n trials and fails several times.   The design flaws causing these failures are corrected, so that the corrected version experiences no failures for the <u>same</u> n trials. It is totally wrong to use the above confidence intervals for the reliability of the corrected version: the claim $p < -\log\alpha/n$ does not reflect $100(1-\alpha)\%$ confidence.

The above analysis can be summarized with a <u>rule</u> <u>of</u> <u>thumb</u>:   To assure a low probability of failure, e.g. $p < 10^{-d}$, requires a string of <u>error-free</u> test cases up to 1 order of magnitude longer than $1/p$, i.e. $n > 10^{d+1/2}$. We saw similar results in the previous section on reliability growth: the amount of testing was much longer than the desired interfailure time.   Combining the results of two statistical analyses like this illustrates the idea of collecting evidence to support a general conclusion. It is difficult to formally combine the two to give one precise conclusion, but numerous results can be informally collected to create quite overwhelming evidence. This approach to statistical analysis is recommended when more formal methods are not available.

The conclusion is that the traditional statistical approach cannot be used to assure ultrahigh levels of reliability because underlying models are not accurate enough and sufficient data cannot be collected. But it may be possible to get a "warm feeling" about the software quality by using an informal "weight of evidence" approach.

BAYESIAN METHODS

We would like to be able to translate everything we know about the software into estimates of how the software performs in the field. There is actually a vast amount of information available and fairly detailed aspects of performance which are of interest. For purposes of statistical reliability analysis, most information is ignored and the performance measure is often reduced to a failure rate. The statistical problem becomes one of estimating future failure rate from observed failures (which could have occurred during development, debugging, testing, or field usage). This is a highly simplified model of the situation, but it is still statistically rich and useful for situations in which sufficient data, i.e., failure data, can be collected.

A Bayesian analysis of the reliability of software is attractive because it provides a way to incorporate more information into the inference. There is a lot of information available in addition to failure data during a software analysis. For example, if the software has been subjected to formal correctness-proving and has survived, this would improve perceived reliability while not guaranteeing perfection. All this information could be incorporated into a prior distribution on the failure rate of the program. However, this only allows escape from huge samples when the software is acceptable a priori. The following example illustrates this: Suppose we assume the prior

$$P(\text{failure rate} = 0) \quad = .99$$
$$P(\text{failure rate} = 10^{-6}) = .01.$$

The prior mean is 10^{-8} which is close to 10^{-9} but not quite acceptable. (Whether the mean is the appropriate measure is another question.) Previously we showed that we wanted an event to be unlikely during 10^8 time units. Consider n test cases without a failure, then

	Bayesian Prior and Posteriors		
n	$P(\text{f.r.}=10^{-6}|\text{Data})$	$E(\text{events in } 10^8)$	$P(0 \text{ events in } 10^8)$
0	.010	1	.368
10^5	.00906	.9	.407
10^6	.00370	.37	.691
10^7	.00000046	.000046	.99995

We see that it is necessary to have a sample that is larger than the MTBF (10^6 executions, in this case) of the bug which may only be present with .01 probability. This illustrates what appears to be a general property of the Bayesian approach: If the software is considered good enough *a priori*, no data are needed. If the software is good enough but the *a priori* feeling is that it is not quite good enough, then a large sample is needed. Such an extreme prior as given here also might not be viewed as credible.

In the above two analyses, a difficulty arises from the two-stage aspect of this problem. The first stage is whether a bug is present. The second stage is whether the bug manifests itself. In the above Bayesian prior distribution we have two possibilities: a perfect program, or a flawed program which we can expect to fail 100 times during the lifetime of the design. If this second possibility occurs, the design will have to be modified, perhaps bankrupting the designer; this has probability .01. It is not clear that the mean of the prior plays a very significant role. A similar two stage feature occurs in the previous confidence interval approach: in this case it can be described in terms of "process" versus "product." The confidence level describes a property of the process of producing or testing software. To say we are 99% confident of having a good piece of software (one with failure rate 10^{-9}) sounds rather strange. A more reasonable statement would be the equivalent one: 99% confidence that the probability of failure during the life of the design is less than .10.

There are at least a couple of specific instances where subjective information can be formally introduced into the software reliability analysis. One involves biasing the random selection of test cases to reflect the tester's feeling that the software is more likely to fail for certain types of inputs. This bias could then be removed from any subsequent reliability estimates.

Another expansion of the purely statistical approach would incorporate any additional information that comes to light when a bug is discovered. The idea is that when a bug manifests itself it usually supplies more information than "error at time t_i." For example, with some thought the programmer may develop a strong feeling for the likelihood that this bug will occur again soon; that is, he may have a better subjective estimate of the failure rate than the estimate that comes from the data (which would be $1/t_i$). He might also realize possibilities of bug interaction that he did not realize before and which are not revealed directly by the data, but which are prompted by consideration of the error caused by the bug. We would like to know if this additional information can be incorporated into a method for reliability assessment, and if so, whether it will improve the assessments. Ross [16] has shown that a special case of this kind of approach will reduce the variance in certain estimates of program failure rate.

There are three main conclusions regarding the Bayesian approach to ultra-high reliability. The prior is very important and huge amounts of data are required to change the prior distribution. The prior distribution is suspect because it is unrealistic to have a precise sense of probabilities related to errors: how can a human have any sense that an error (that he didn't think of) will manifest itself with probability 10^{-9} instead of 10^{-7}, say. Finally, because of the first two conclusions, a formal Bayesian analysis is not a realistic software quality assurance method. This realization has strong implications challenging the qualitative approach to software quality assurance, because the qualitative approach is an informal subjective methodology.

USING STRUCTURAL MODELS

Structural models can be useful in predicting (or assuring) system performance. However, models are based on assumptions and may need parameter values. If these assumptions are only approximately true and the parameter values must be estimated, then the model may not be precise enough for high reliability applications. Validation of the model may require more extensive testing than would be required for more straightforward reliability estimation based on a black-box model. We illustrate this point with a model of n-version fault-tolerant software.

There are two aspects of high reliability for safety-critical applications: achievement and verification. Fault tolerance has been used successfully to achieve very high levels of reliability; see the recent Proceedings of the International Symposium on Fault-Tolerant Computing [3]. One approach to software fault tolerance is n-version software. This allows for higher system design reliability than that of individual components. Thus, if higher software reliability is sought by using n-version programming, we should also be able to exploit this fact in assuring reliability. However, we encounter the problem that separate software components do not *a priori* fail independently (as is sometimes assumed in hardware models). Eckhardt and Lee [4] have shown theoretically why independence fails, and Knight and Leveson [8] have shown experimentally that programs which are independently created will show dependencies in failing.

Consider a two-out-of-three software system in which three independently created versions of the software perform the same computational tasks and then use a flawless majority voter. Let F_S denote system failure and F_i denote failure of the ith component, i = 1,2,3; then

$$P(F_S) = P(F_1 \cap F_2) + P(F_1 \cap F_3) + P(F_2 \cap F_3)$$
$$- 2P(F_1 \cap F_2 \cap F_3)$$

This may be manipulated into an equivalent expression:

$$P(F_S) = P(F_1)P(F_2) + P(F_1)P(F_3) + P(F_2)P(F_3)$$
$$- 2P(F_1)P(F_2)P(F_3) + (P(F_1 \cap F_2) - P(F_1)P(F_2))$$
$$+ (P(F_1 \cap F_3) - P(F_1)P(F_3)) + (P(F_2 \cap F_3) - P(F_2)P(F_3))$$
$$- 2(P(F_1 \cap F_2 \cap F_3) - P(F_1)P(F_2)P(F_3))$$

In the second expression for $P(F_S)$ the last four terms are covariances which disappear if the three versions fail independently of one another. (The interpretation of these terms as "covariances" can be seen by considering the random variables X_1, X_2, and X_3, where $X_i = 1$ if component i fails and $X_i = 0$ otherwise. By definition, $Cov(X_1, X_2) = E(X_1X_2 - EX_1EX_2) = EX_1X_2 - EX_1EX_2 = P(X_1X_2 = 1) - P(X_1 = 1)P(X_2 = 1) = P(F_1 \cap F_2) - P(F_1)P(F_2)$.) If independence cannot be assumed these covariance terms must be estimated or bounded in some way. The difficulty is that in order for the three-version system to be a significant improvement over the one-version system, the covariance terms must be very close to zero and this must be verified in order to verify the system reliability. So we must verify that

$$P(F_i \cap F_j) < 10^{-9}$$

Hence we are back to the original problem which requires a huge sample, accurate knowledge of the usage domain and distribution, and so on. Any statistical approach that claims to support ultrareliability based on a moderate amount of data is almost certainly based on assumptions; verification of these assumptions would require a huge amount of data.

Another type of structural model of software has been proposed by Littlewood [9]. The software consists of modules and interfaces. The execution path through the software consists of sojourns within modules and transitions between modules according to a continuous time Markov chain. Failures occur according to Poisson processes within modules and Bernoulli processes at interfaces. This is an excellent high-level model for very large systems of reliable modules with nominal system reliability. But to validate this model and estimate the parameter values for assurance of ultrahigh reliability would again probably require as much test data as the black-box approach to quality assurance. Models can be used to gain insight and understanding of failure phenomena but not to circumvent the statistical axiom that "you don't get something for nothing."

FORMAL SOFTWARE DEVELOPMENT METHODS

The goal of formal software development methods is to create higher quality software. The ultimate goal of methods such as "correctness-proving" techniques is to create software without design flaws. These methods have improved the quality of software and have the potential to achieve even higher quality. If they are completely successful then quality assurance based on testing will be unnecessary; the quality of the software will be assured as perfect. There are two major shortcomings of the formal "proof-of-correctness" approach: the technique does not cover the entire system, and past experience with the method has included incorrect "proofs."

Formal methods are not applied to the entire system. Generally formal methods are used to guarantee correct implementation of a formal specification. The specification may not be correct or may be ambiguous. Furthermore, in practice, producing a specification whose implementation is amenable to formal proof may favor that part of the overall system at the expense of other parts of the system, increasing the chance of design errors in these other parts.

Another problem with formal methods is that there are documented cases of software which has been "proven" correct and later found to not perform as intended. Thus, the possibility of system design errors existing in "proven" software must be conceded. This concession puts us back into the realm of "uncertainty:" the software either is correct or it isn't, and we don't know which. The quantitative approach to this dilemma is again the statistical approach.

Here is a crude statistical analysis of assurance of software which has been proven correct: We are skeptical because we know of past failures of the method; so we believe there is a possibility that the software contains a design flaw which will eventually manifest itself as a failure. Let q equal the probability that a program developed with current state-of-the-art proof methods is imperfect. Suppose there have been n "similar" software projects developed since this technique has been perfected. Further suppose that these n projects have now accumulated extensive real-world use without any design errors being discovered. This situation is statistically identical to the previous situation with unknown probability p of software failing in a given random trial. So a $100(1-\alpha)\%$ confidence interval for q is

$$q \leq q_\alpha = -\log\alpha/n$$

If $n=100$, we are 99% confident that $q \leq .046$, i.e. the new software is flawed with probability at most .046. This analysis is very crude. (It should strike the reader as being somewhat ludicrous.) The idea of "similar" projects is too vague. It does show, however, in light of earlier false "proofs," that the methodology needs a long string of successes in order to redeem itself. In fact, reliability growth modelling could be applied to the improvement in this method over successive projects. However, the necessary quantum jump in belief that the method creates very good software to the belief that it creates perfect software may be impossible.

Note that the above parameter q is a characteristic of the software development process and does not describe an individual piece of software. A low value for q gives assurance about the quality of the software development process.

ASSURING THE DEVELOPMENT PROCESS

It is hard, or impossible, to assure ultrareliability of individual pieces of software in a quantitative or statistical sense. Assurance in a qualitative sense in practice is usually assurance that "good" software development methods were properly used. In effect, the development process is assured to be of high quality; the actual software produced may never be examined.

The qualitative approach to assuring a software development process is a rather arbitrary and subjective procedure. Acceptable methods (perhaps the waterfall model of development) are identified. The type and amount of documentation for a single application is specified. After development the project is, in effect, audited. Then a judgment is rendered. This type of assurance procedure is performed for each software system. The actual software may then be certified. As certified software becomes more and more prevalent, sufficient data for statistical scrutiny will become available. Management of this data base and making inferences from it will be important roles for statistical methods. It may be possible retroactively to assess success or failure of assurance and certification activities.

An important consideration when assuring or certifying a software development process is the fact that different software produced using the same development method can have considerable variability. For example, the 27 versions produced in an experiment conducted by Knight and Leveson [8] showed tremendous variability in reliability. It is safe to say that any development method properly used can still produce levels of quality ranging from acceptable to unacceptable software. For this reason, assurance of the process appears to be risky and perhaps not even quantifiable.

A quantitative approach to assurance of a software development process would be a huge undertaking involving many individual projects, and the collection and analysis of as much data as possible. Dramatic advances in the field of software metrics would help. A good beginning would be controlled experimentation on software development and testing such as NASA is supporting, e.g. [4, 13, 14]. Still, it is hard to imagine any quantitative assurances that a development process produces ultrareliable software. The main role for statistics in this arena may be to counter outrageous assurance claims.

ENGINEERING PRACTICE

A formal, quantitative, scientific approach to assuring the quality of software which must be ultrareliable is not available. In practice, attempts at assurance are made in different ways. When these more qualitative approaches are examined from a quantitative point of view, some contradictions are uncovered.

Consider the following scenario: We wish to assure the reliability of a software system to a very high level of reliability, say 10^{-9} probability of failure per mission. The software is developed using the best available software engineering techniques. The programmers are highly skilled and follow the development guidelines properly. All the functions of the software are carefully tested. The software is tested in simulated real-world usage equivalent to 100,000 randomly chosen missions and no failures are observed. (If any failures had been observed the entire project would have to be declared a failure with no salvage value.) Careful and complete documentation is compiled. The entire project is carefully scrutinized and no shortcomings are detected. Finally, the software is declared acceptable at the desired level of reliability and certified.

Here is the reaction to the above scenario from a statistical point of view: The random testing in a simulated real-world usage environment is illogical! This test data only assures the failure probability in a range, $p < 10^{-4.5}$. (To be confident that $p < 10^{-9}$ would require at least 10^9 test cases without failure.) One billion test cases have been avoided (at huge cost savings). In effect, good engineering has replaced extensive testing. The testing will catch any high-frequency bugs. So, the good engineering must prevent low frequency bugs. But, if good engineering can do this, it can also prevent high-frequency bugs from occurring. So the testing was a total waste of time and resources.

A more tempered reaction to the above scenario is that such assurances have been proven valid after the fact. There is strong intuition that the random simulated real-world testing is an important aspect of the assurance process. Thus, the above criticism may reflect incomplete understanding of the process. An important role for statistical methods is to analyze the process, to get a better quantitative understanding of it.

The character of actual engineering practice is beautifully described by Henry Petroski in his book To Engineer is Human [15]. Although he focuses on structures in civil engineering, the observations are valid for engineering design in general. He emphasizes the subjective aspect of new designs, trial-and-error, and learning more from failures than from successes. From the historical perspective of this book, the *a priori* assurance of ultrahigh reliability of new designs based on formal scientific quantitative methods is a new requirement. It has never really been done before. But since each new piece of software can be viewed as a new design, we are faced with an explosion of new designs. So perhaps the time has come to require better assurance practices.

PUBLIC PRONOUNCEMENTS AND PERCEPTIONS

In the software development arena there exist pressures to make optimistic, exaggerated, or unsupported claims about system quality. The Advanced Automation System (AAS) under development by the U.S. Federal Aviation Administration provides some examples which may reflect this. The February 1987 issue of Computer is devoted to the FAA's Advanced Automation Program.

The Area Control Computer Coupler (ACCC) is the central component of the AAS. The ACCC must meet extremely high availability requirements if the system is to operate safely. Avizienis and Ball [1] state the availability requirements for different operational modes:

Availability Requirements for ACCC

Operational mode	Goal	Requirement	
Full-Service	1.0	.999995	(2.6 min/yr)
Reduced capacity	1.0	.999999	(32 sec/yr)
Emergency	1.0	.9999999	(3 sec/yr)

where the parenthetic expressions are the equivalent allowable times of system unavailability. When such high availability is required, design (or software) reliability must be considered.

Avizienis and Ball [1] appear to say that analytical models will be used in the verification of the ultrareliability of fault-tolerance in the AAS. This claim is not supported; it seems to be based on the assumption that such models are exact rather than approximate.

On July 27, 1988, the Washington Post quoted Mr. Gerry Ebker, Vice President of

IBM, concerning the AAS for which IBM won the FAA contract. He said, "The system has the capability to stay on line for all but a few seconds per year." It is not clear how to interpret this statement. The implication is that the actual system will meet the specified requirements.

It is not clear how the public perceives these systems which are so highly touted. Although the burden for proper quality assurance should rest with the developer and promoters of these systems, some sort of independent consumer advocacy and protection is required. Statistical methods can be used to reveal unsupported claims of assurance.

ROLES FOR STATISTICS IN ASSURANCE AND CERTIFICATION

Unfortunately the statistical method cannot provide a formal, rigorous, scientific approach which will assure ultrahigh levels of software reliability. But there are several auxiliary and peripheral roles it should take:

i)   Assuring or warranting systems which aspire to only moderate levels of reliability. See Currit, Dyer and Mills [2] for an example.

ii)   Use in controlled experiments to investigate and gain understanding of software engineering phenomena.

iii)   Investigate quality achievement *a posteriori*.

iv)   Weapon to attack outlandish *a priori* claims of assurance of high reliability and safety.

v)   A framework within which to precisely define concepts of uncertainty - even in nonquantifiable situations.

CONCLUSIONS

It is difficult to prove something is impossible, but the evidence suggests that a formal statistical verification of reliability will be impossible for many safety critical systems. The best software development and evaluation techniques will be used and huge amounts of documentation, as well as extensive testing, will be required for certification. But it is unlikely that this can be formed into a statistically rigorous verification. It is also fairly certain that such systems will be built. On the other hand, systems (such as bridges) have been built which turned out to be ultrareliable *a posteriori*. The *a priori* assurance seems more elusive than the achievement of ultrareliability.

ACKNOWLEDGMENTS

This research was supported by the National Aeronautics and Space Administration, Grant NAG 1-771. Various people read earlier drafts of this paper and contributed useful comments; they include Ricky Butler, Mike DeWalt, Janet Dunham, George Finelli, Kelly Hayhurst, Bev Littlewood, and Earle Migneault.

REFERENCES

1. Avizeinis, A. and Ball, D. E., On the achievement of a highly dependable and fault-tolerant air traffic system, Computer, February 1987, 20(2), 84-90.

2. Currit, P. A., Dyer, M. and Mills, H. D., Certifying the reliability of software, IEEE Transactions on Software Engineering, 1986, SE-12, 3-11.

3. Digest of Papers: 16th Annual International Symposium on Fault-Tolerant Computing, IEEE Computer Society Press, Washington, D.C. 1986.

4. Dunham, J. R., Experiment in software reliability: life-critical applications, IEEE Transactions on Software Engineering, 1986, SE-12, 110-123.

5. Eckhardt, D. E. and Lee, L. D., A theoretical basis for the analysis of multiversion software subject to coincident errors, IEEE Transactions on Software Engineering, 1985, SE-11, 1511-1517.

6. Federal Aviation Administration, System design analysis, Advisory Circular AC-25.1309-1, U.S. Department of Transportation, September 7, 1982.

7. Jelinski, Z. and Moranda, P. B., Software reliability research, Statistical Computer Performance Evaluation (W. Freiberger, ed.), Academic Press, Inc., New York, 1972, 464-484.

8. Knight, J. C. and Leveson, N. G., An experimental evaluation of the assumption of independence in multiversion programming, IEEE Transactions on Software Engineering, 1986, SE-12, 96-109.

9. Littlewood, B., A reliability model for systems with markov structure, Applied Statistics, 1975, 24, 172-177.

10. Littlewood, B., Discussion at IEEE Computer Society Workshop on Laboratories for Reliable Systems Research, NASA Langley Research Center, October 1983.

11. Miller, D. R., Exponential order statistic models of software reliability growth, IEEE Transactions on Software Engineering, 1986, SE-12, 12-24.

12. Musa, J. D., Software Reliability Data. Bell Telephone Laboratories. Whippany, N.J., 1979.

13. Nagel, P. M., Scholz, F. W. and Skrivan, J. A., Software reliability: additional investigations into modeling with replicated experiments, NASA CR-172378, 1984.

14. Nagel, P. M. and Skrivan, J. A., Software reliability: repetitive run experimentation and modeling, NASA CR-165836, 1982.

15. Petroski, H., To Engineer is Human: The Role of Failure in Successful Design, St. Martin's Press, New York, 1985.

16. Ross, S. M., Statistical estimation of software reliability, IEEE Transactions on Software Engineering, 1985, SE-11, 479-483.

17. Scholz, F. -W., Software reliability modeling and analysis, IEEE Transactions on Software Engineering, 1986, SE-12, 25-31.

18. Special Committee 152, Software considerations in airborne systems and equipment certification, Radio Technical Commission for Aeronautics, DO-178A, Washington, D.C., March 1985.

11

THE ROLE OF FORMAL MATHEMATICS IN THE ASSURANCE OF SOFTWARE

Bernard de Neumann

Department of Mathematics
& Centre for Software Reliability,
City University,
Northampton Square, LONDON, EC1V 0HB, UK.

ABSTRACT

The Formal Methods of Software Engineering, which are a major
feature of present research, place heavy reliance upon the
traditional, formal practices of mathematics (albeit augmented
by the use of computers). Whilst not decrying these
approaches, this paper will discuss some of the inherent
problems of these mathematical methodologies. It is intended
to demonstrate, that whilst these techniques can undoubtedly
be relied upon to overcome some types of error, there are
other areas in which no such assurance can be obtained from
them. These limitations will impact upon the reliability of a
product, and hence in the cases where certification is a
requirement, such considerations should influence heavily the
methods to be used to assess the fitness of the item to be
certified.

INTRODUCTION

The axioms of a mathematical theory essentially specify a
particular system for consideration. Note that throughout
this paper we shall treat the terms 'axiomatic theory' and
'axiomatic system' synonymously. Mathematicians who work in
this field use certain criteria for the selection of
interesting systems, and further other criteria for assessing
the 'elegance' of the axioms and resulting theorems.

Experience of such axiomatic systems has taught mathematicians to exercise caution, and it has become customary in mathematics to also attempt to demonstrate that axioms describe non-vacuous and non-contradictory (consistent) systems. It seems natural to make the analogy between formal functional specifications for software, and the formal axiomatic methods of mathematics. Clearly both are concerned with specifying abstractions which have only logical and mathematical properties. Furthermore the relationships of such systems with other such systems, and in particular their relationship with the current abstraction which goes under the guise of the 'real world', is a matter of interpretation. This question of interpretation could be of the greatest significance in the safety/certification field, however we do not intend to treat it here.

AXIOMATICS

The methodology of axiomatics is enacted by introducing:

(1) a set of <u>primitive symbols</u> which of necessity are not rigorously defined,

(2) a set of <u>defined symbols</u> defined in terms of the primitive symbols, and

(3) a <u>logic</u> to deduce theorems about the system.

To illustrate this we give as an example an axiomatic basis for group theory.

(1) Primitive Set = an unspecified set G, together with a binary operation on pairs of elements of G denoted by: a.b for $a, b \in G$ which is a function on $G \times G$ into G.

(2) Axioms (defined set) =
  G1 $\forall a, b, c \in G$ $a.(b.c) = (a.b).c$

G2 $\forall a \, \varepsilon \, G \qquad a.e = e.a = a$

G3 For each $a \, \varepsilon \, G \, \exists a' \, \varepsilon \, G$ s. th. $a.a' = a'.a = e$

In order to reduce the defined symbols it is customary to use the existing, and well-known nomenclature of mathematics.

A less familiar example of an axiomatic system (1) is given in the appendix. In fact this example was the first instance of a geometry in which the concept of a point was not fundamental.

Mathematicians have studied axiomatic systems per se since roughly the beginning of the twentieth century, and during this time have made a number of important discoveries. These have irreversibly changed the outlook of mathematics, as well as highlighting the limitations, and strengths of the axiomatic approach. What then do mathematicians look for in a set of axioms? How can such properties assist software engineers? It is, it should be stressed, important to realise that a 'theory' is not necessarily based upon a unique set of axioms. For example Euclidean Geometry has had several axiomatic bases proposed over the last two thousand years.

The properties that have been identified thus far, as being of importance to axiomatic mathematical theories are as follows:

* CONCISENESS - Small number of axioms (minimal number).

* CONSISTENCY - It is not possible to derive a contradiction by assuming the axioms are true.

* COMPLETENESS - The axioms together completely specify the theory.

* INDEPENDENCE - No axiom is derivable from the others.

* CATEGORICALNESS - All interpretations of the axiomatic theory are equivalent. (Categoricalness implies completeness.)

* EQUIVALENCE - Two axiomatic systems are equivalent if each implies the other.

The notion of completeness as stated above contains an element of latitude and so the notion can be further refined as follows:

(1) A theory Υ is <u>deductively complete</u> if, and only if, every valid statement of Υ is provable. (A valid statement is true in every model.)

(2) A theory Υ is <u>formally complete</u> if any theory Υ' formed by adding a statement of Υ which is not a theorem to Υ is inconsistent.

(3) A theory Υ is <u>negation complete</u> if, for any statement A of Υ, either A or $\sim$A is a theorem.

In order to clarify the notion of categoricalness, we state the following. A set of axioms $P = \{P_1, P_2, P_3, \ldots P_n\}$ connecting a set of undefined objects $S = \{S_1, S_2, \ldots S_m\}$ is said to be <u>categorical</u> if between the elements of any two assemblages, each of which contains undefined symbols and satisfies the axioms, it is possible to set up a one-to-one correspondence of the undefined concepts which is preserved by the relationships asserted by the axioms; that is the two systems are isomorphic. In effect, all interpretations of the axiom system differ only by language.

Of course the study of axiomatic systems per se goes back to Hilbert at the beginning of the twentieth century. Hilbert's attempt to show that all of mathematics is consistent and complete, his Beweistheorie, was demolished by Gödel's famous incompleteness (undecidability) result (2). Hilbert's work, and that of his students, was directed towards transfinite systems, in order to overcome certain difficulties which had arisen. Couched in these terms, finite systems, and, inter alia, computer science and software engineering, are trivial!

Thus it has taken some 2000 years for mathematics to achieve its present state of understanding in axiomatics, most of which development took place in the last 50 years or so. Some limitations have become apparent in this latter period, and the corpus of experience so obtained may well be of utility to the software engineering fraternity. We therefore propose to discuss the important common notions of axiomatic theories, as described above, with regard to their potential importance to software engineering.

MATHEMATICAL AXIOMATICS AND THE FORMAL METHODS OF SOFTWARE ENGINEERING

In the previous section we have briefly described the notions of axiomatic systems which mathematicians have found to be important. We now intend to assess their relevance to the formal methods of Software Engineering, especially with regard to formal functional specification, although the same criteria should also apply to any formal specification. An important distinction potentially lies in the number of axioms typically studied in a mathematical axiomatic theory, compared with the typical number of statements in a formal functional specification. (Of course such a size metric has all of the drawbacks which are known to exist, for example, for 'number of lines of code', the metric so beloved of software cost estimators.) Typical mathematical axiomatic systems have of the order of 5 to 20 axioms (10 say), whereas for the typical formal specifications which we anticipate the number of statements to be of the order of 10^4 to 10^6 (10^5 say).

* CONCISENESS - Brevity has always been of interest to mathematicians, who often equate brevity with elegance. Their activities in this direction are essentially experimental, and the degree of conciseness a matter of taste. Of course the

mathematical motivation for this is partly due to a fear that too many axioms could lead to inconsistency. It is difficult to see how such a process may be automated for the purposes of Software Engineering. Furthermore it could be that prolixity, provided that it is consistent, could even be beneficial to software engineering insofar as some redundancy in specification could provide some protection against errors (3).

* INDEPENDENCE - Mathematicians demonstrate the independence of axioms by constructing models (consistent interpretations) of subsets of the axioms. This activity is important to mathematicians in their quest for conciseness, and the elimination of unnecessary axioms. It is not at all evident that independence is a desirable attribute for statements in a software specification. Indeed in the case of software engineering, 'non-independence', or at least 'almost dependence' could have application in the formal specification of fault tolerant multi-version software. Furthermore we should recognise that the potential for making mistakes in formal specifications containing, of necessity, large numbers of statements, is very great. It thus seems natural to advocate the use of fault tolerant multi-version formal specifications. Recent work (4) has shown that fault tolerant multi-version software is most likely to be reliable if there is a strong negative correlation between versions. It is worth remarking that, for a system containing n axioms/statements, the total number of subsets of two or more axioms/statements is equal to $2^n - n - 1$. Thus using our figures from above, the task of showing the independence of a typical formal specification is $O(2^{49990} = 10^{30100})$ times harder than that of showing the independence of a mathematical system.

* CONSISTENCY - The mathematical demonstration of consistency is very difficult. For example, Hilbert, at the beginning of the twentieth century, showed that Euclidean Geometry is consistent if arithmetic is consistent. In fact

we still do not know if arithmetic is consistent, although most mathematicians tacitly accept that it is. In their task of proving the independence of the Axiom of Choice in Set Theory, Gödel (5) and Cohen (6) demonstrated the consistency of the other axioms by showing the existence of two non-vacuous models for a set theory, one, assuming that the axiom of choice is true, and the other, assuming that the axiom of choice is false. The fact that thirty years elapsed between Gödel's work and Cohen's complementary work is a measure of the difficulty of proving consistency. For software engineering, consistency of the specification is obviously of paramount importance. Yet, even for 'simple' mathematical systems (with relatively few axioms/statements), we hardly know how to progress, and, in view of the time-lapse in Gödel's and Cohen's work, how can we expect to deal with our typical formal specification in a realistic time? In fact, if we suppose that a realistic time for proving consistency is of the order of weeks, then our result, above, shows that we need an improvement in efficiency over first-rank mid-twentieth century mathematicians of 10^{30103} times! Whilst the increase in efficiency of computers up to the present time has been spectacular, it in no way matches the improvement required to implement the above performance. Proof of consistency appears to be a skilful and entirely intellectual activity, and in view of the above result, it is likely to remain so for some considerable time to come. Probably because of the intellectual content of consistency proofs, existing computer theorem provers tacitly assume consistency in their given axioms. This is extremely dangerous, particularly since, at least some, existing automatic theorem provers have to, on occasions, when they cannot, in a realistic time, either prove or disprove a desired result, accept as true a humanly affirmed statement; This is then treated as an essentially new axiom.

* COMPLETENESS - It seems obvious that any system should be completely specified, yet it is the case that most software specifications are incomplete - insofar as they often

tend to concentrate upon the main (positive) functions of a
system, and it is tacitly left to the programmer to decide
what to do in other cases, often based upon his common sense
notions of what the customer could reasonably expect.   For
mathematics Gödel's famous Incompleteness Theorem precludes
the demonstration of completeness for any formal system
capable of embracing number theory.   For software engineering
this is not a problem since finite-state machines are not
capable of representing mathematical number theory.
Furthermore, in principle at least, it is possible to
enumerate all possible input-output cases for a finite-state
machine. However such an approach is rarely practical. Also
it is worth stating the obvious mathematical fact that a
finite number of axioms/statements does not necessarily lead
to a complete specification.   The work of Chaitin (7) on
algorithmic computational complexity is also of relevance
here. He defines the algorithmic computational complexity of
an arbitrary string to be the length of the minimal input
string to a particular universal Turing machine which enables
that machine to compute the original string.   Thus, for us,
the algorithmic complexity of a completely specified system is
bounded from above by the length of the input-output string.
Unfortunately Chaitin proved that most strings have complexity
of the order of the length of the string.

  * CATEGORICALNESS   -   The   assurance   of   a   unique
interpretation of a set of specification statements seems to
be of particular importance to software engineering.   This is
especially true when one considers the scope for disaster if
ambiguity is possible in a specification.   This condition is
also dangerous in the integration phase - safe subsystems can
be linked to produce unsafe systems: Thus interface
specification is also important.   Note that mathematically,
CATEGORICALNESS implies COMPLETENESS, but COMPLETENESS does
not imply CATEGORICALNESS.   CATEGORICALNESS is also known as
CATEGORICITY.   Note that a categorical specification is also
complete.

* EQUIVALENCE - Prima facie this is not a particularly interesting property, since, ostensibly, any equivalent categorical specifications will result in a unique, from the input-output point of view, system. However given the human being's propensity for making errors, and in view of the remarks under the headings of Conciseness and Independence above, it is entirely possible that (attempted) equivalence by means of some system of complementary specifications could be a valuable approach.

To reiterate: For Software Engineering; Conciseness is probably of little importance, although some effort in that direction may be appropriate; Independence per se is probably irrelevant; Consistency, Completeness, and Categoricalness are all of the utmost importance; and Equivalence, Conciseness, and Independence, when taken together could be of importance in order to produce fault tolerant specifications.

CONCLUSIONS

The general principles of mathematical axiomatics have been discussed in terms of their potential application to formal functional specifications. It has been shown that at least some of the concepts discovered by mathematicians in this field are of consequence, and that the experience of these mathematicians can only be ignored at the peril of society.

If Software Engineering is to mature, so that it is possible to produce meaningfully certifiable software/systems at some future date using formal methods, then we must research means to improve our ability to attack systems with large numbers of specification statements/axioms. In essence we need the ability to 'engineer' (in its original sense) such systems, and manipulate them, and adapt them to our needs. In the author's opinion the trend is such that, eventually, all engineering will be subordinated to the prior manipulation of abstract objects which have only logical and mathematical properties. This prior manipulation, which is in a sense applied axiomatics, may perhaps be termed integrated theoretical engineering, or information engineering, and may involve the extensive development of Integrated Systems Factories, and Integrated Product Support Environments (IPSEs).

Of course, compliance with the existing principles of mathematical axiomatcs will in no way guarentee that a specification is correct (viz. as intended): A certified correct and safe avionics system, say, will probably not open a can of worms - or maybe it will!

REFERENCES

1. Neumann, J. von, Continuous Geometry, Oxford U. P., 1960.

2. Gödel, K., On Formally Undecidable Propositions of Principia Mathematica and Related Systems. In The Undecidable, ed. M. Davis, Raven Press, 1965.

3. Neumann, B de, Entropy/Information Theory and (Software) Reliability. In Software Reliability: Achievement and Assessment, ed. B. Littlewood, Blackwell Sc. Pub., 1987, pp. 167-171.

4. Littlewood, B. and Miller, D.R., A Conceptual Model of Multi-Version Software. In Digest of the 17th International Fault-Tolerant Computing Symposium, Pittsburgh, 1987, pp. 150-155

5. Godel, K., The Consistency of the Axiom of Choice...., Princeton U. P., 1940.

6. Cohen, P., Set Theory and the Continuum Hypothesis, Benjamin, 1966.

7. Chaitin, G., <u>Algorithmic Information Theory</u>, Cambridge U. P., 1987.

APPENDIX

EXAMPLE OF AN AXIOMATIC SYSTEM

Basis of development is a <u>set</u> L of elements a,b,c... two or more in number, together with a binary <u>relation</u> < between pairs of elements of L.

The elements of L and the relation < are <u>undefined</u>.

Together with the above are given the axioms which specify the properties of the system.

AXIOM I: Order.

I_1 : a < a for no a ε L.

I_2 : a < b < c $\Rightarrow$ a < c.

DEFINITION 1: a > b means b < a: a $\leq$ b means a < b or a = b; a $\geq$ b means b $\leq$ a.

AXIOM II: Continuity.

II_1 : For every $S \subset L$, there is an element $\Sigma(s)$ in L, which is a <u>least upper bound</u> of S, ie

(a) $\Sigma(s) \geqslant a \ \forall a \varepsilon S$

(b) $x \geqslant a \ \text{for every} \ a \varepsilon S \ \Rightarrow \ x \geqslant \Sigma(s)$

II_2 : For every $S \subset L$, there is an element $\Pi(s)$ in L, which is a <u>greatest lower bound</u> of S, ie

(a) $\Pi(s) \leq a \ \forall a \varepsilon S$

(b) $x \leq a \ \text{for every} \ a \varepsilon S \ \Rightarrow \ x \leq \Pi(s)$

COROLLARY: $\Sigma(s)$ and $\Pi(s)$ are unique.

PROOF: If $\Sigma_1(s)$, $\Sigma_2(s)$ satisfy (a) and (b) of II_1, then since $\Sigma_1(s)$ satisfies (a) and $\Sigma_2(s)$ satisfies (b), we have $\Sigma_1(s) \geqslant \Sigma_2(s)$

Similarly $\Sigma_1(s) \leq \Sigma_2(s)$

If $\Sigma_1(s) \neq \Sigma_2(s)$, we have both $\Sigma_1(s) > \Sigma_2(s)$ and $\Sigma_1(s) < \Sigma_2(s)$

so I_2 implies $\Sigma_1(s) < \Sigma_1(s)$, which contradicts I_1. In a similar way $\Pi(s)$ may be proved to be unique.

DEFINITION 2: The elements $\Pi(L)$, $\Sigma(L)$ will be denoted by 0, 1 respectively. It follows from II_1, (b) and II_2, (b) that if ϕ is the empty subset of L, $0 = \Sigma(\phi)$, $1 = \Pi(\phi)$.

DEFINITION 3: Let (a,b) denote the set consisting of the elements a,b. Then we define

$$a+b \equiv \Sigma(a,b) \qquad ab \equiv a.b \equiv \Pi(a,b)$$

COROLLARY: a+a = a, aa = a.

DEFINITION 4: Let Ω be any infinite Cantor $\aleph$. Let there be a system of elements $(a_\alpha, \alpha < \Omega)$. We consider only two cases

(i) $\alpha < \beta \Rightarrow a_\alpha \leq a_\beta$

(ii) $\alpha < \beta \Rightarrow a_\alpha \geq a_\beta$

In case (i) we define

$$\lim_{\alpha \to \Omega}{}^* a_\alpha \equiv \Sigma(a_\alpha ; \alpha < \Omega)$$

where the RHS denotes the lub of the set of all a ;
In case (ii) we define

$$\lim_{\alpha \to \Omega}{}^* a_\alpha \equiv \Pi(a_\alpha ; \alpha < \Omega)$$

COROLLARY: Let (a_α) be a system satisfying (i). Then for every b, the system $(b+a_\alpha)$ satisfies (i) and

$$\lim_{\alpha \to \Omega}{}^* (b + a_\alpha) = b + \lim_{\alpha \to \Omega}{}^* (a_\alpha)$$

Similarly if (a_α) satisfies (ii), (ba_α) satisfies (ii) and

$$\lim_{\alpha \to \Omega}{}^* (ba_\alpha) = b \lim_{\alpha \to \Omega}{}^* (a_\alpha)$$

PROOF: The proof is quite long, and immaterial to this paper, so we shall not give it here.

AXIOM III: Continuity of addition and multiplication

III_1 : Let Ω be an infinite $\aleph$ and $(a_\alpha ; \alpha < \Omega)$ a system satisfying (ii) of Definition 4. Then

$$\lim_{\alpha \to \Omega}{}^* (b + a_\alpha) = b + \lim_{\alpha \to \Omega}{}^* (a_\alpha)$$

III$_2$: Let Ω be an infinite $\aleph$ and $(a_\alpha; \alpha < \Omega)$ a system satisfying (i) of Definition 4. Then

$$\lim_{\alpha \to \Omega}{}^* (b a_\alpha) = b \lim_{\alpha \to \Omega}{}^* a_\alpha$$

AXIOM IV: Modularity

     IV$_1$: $a \leqslant c \Rightarrow (a+b)c = a+bc, \forall b$

AXIOM V: Complementation

     V$_1$: Corresponding to each $a \varepsilon$ L, $\exists x \varepsilon$ L s. th. $a+x = 1$, $ax = 0$.

AXIOM VI: Irreducibility

     VI$_1$: If a has a unique inverse, then a is either 0 or 1.

INDEX